KU-157-706

118

American Poetry

American Poetry

An Introductory Anthology

Edited with an Introduction by
DONALD HALL

STIRLING
DISTRICT
LIBRARY

FABER AND FABER
24 Russell Square
London

879909

811
HAL

First published in 1969
by Faber and Faber Limited
24 Russell Square London WC1
Printed in Great Britain
by Ebenezer Baylis & Son, Ltd
The Trinity Press, Worcester, and London
All rights reserved

SBN 571 08704 3 (cloth edition)
SBN 571 08981 X (paperback edition)

Introduction © Donald Hall 1969
This selection © Faber and Faber 1969

Acknowledgements

For permission to reprint copyright material, the following acknowledgements are made:

For poems by Earle Birney, from *Selected Poems* by Earle Birney, reprinted by permission of the Canadian Publishers, McClelland and Stewart Limited, Toronto.

For a poem by Elizabeth Bishop, to the author and to Chatto and Windus, Ltd., from her book, *Poems*.

For poems by John Berryman, to the author and Faber and Faber, Ltd.

For poems by E. E. Cummings, to MacGibbon & Kee, Ltd., from *The Complete Poems of E. E. Cummings*.

For poems by Hart Crane, from *The Collected Poems of Hart Crane*. By permission of Liveright Publishers, N.Y. Copyright © 1961 by Liveright Publishing Corporation.

For poems by Emily Dickinson, to the Harvard University Press and Little, Brown and Co. Reprinted by permission of the publishers and Trustees of Amherst College from Thomas H. Johnson, Editor, *The Poems of Emily Dickinson*, Cambridge, Mass.: The Belknap Press of Harvard University Press, Copyright © 1951, 1955, by the President and Fellows of Harvard College. From *The Complete Poems of Emily Dickinson*, edited by Thomas H. Johnson, by permission of Little, Brown: 'After great pain, a formal feeling comes', Copyright, 1929, © 1957, by Mary L. Hampson. 'A little madness in the spring', Copyright, 1914, 1942, by Martha Dickinson Bianchi.

For poems by Richard Eberhart, to the author and to Chatto and Windus, Ltd., from *Collected Poems*.

For poems by H. D., to Grove Press, Inc. Copyright © 1957 by Norman Holmes Pearson.

For poems by Robert Frost, to Laurence Pollinger Ltd., Jonathan Cape Ltd., and Holt, Rinehart and Winston. 'The Draft Horse', from *In the Clearing* by Robert Frost, Copyright © 1962 by Robert Frost. Reprinted by permission of Holt, Rinehart and Winston, Inc., Publishers, New York.

For poems by Robinson Jeffers, to Random House, Inc.

For poems by Robert Lowell, to Faber and Faber, Ltd.

For poems by Irving Layton, from *A Red Carpet for the Sun* by Irving Layton, by permission of the Canadian Publishers, McClelland and Stewart Limited, Toronto.

For poems by Vachel Lindsay, to the Meredith Press and the Macmillan Company. 'The Flower-Fed Buffaloes', Copyright, 1926, by D. Appleton & Co., Copyright renewed, 1954, by Elizabeth C. Lindsay. 'Factory Windows are Always Broken', reprinted by permission of The Macmillan Company from *The Congo and Other Poems* by Vachel Lindsay, Copyright 1914 by The Macmillan Company, renewed 1942 by Elizabeth C. Lindsay.

For poems by Edgar Lee Masters, from *Spoon River Anthology*, to Mrs. Edgar Lee Masters.

For poems by Marianne Moore, to Faber and Faber, Ltd.

For a poem by Archibald MacLeish, from *Collected Poems*, to Houghton Mifflin Co.

For poems by Ezra Pound, to Faber and Faber, Ltd.

For poems by E. J. Pratt, from *Collected Poems*, to Macmillan & Co., Ltd.

For a poem by Phelps Putnam, to Una W. Putnam.

For poems by John Crowe Ransom, to Laurence Pollinger Ltd., Eyre and Spottiswoode, Ltd., and Alfred A. Knopf, Inc.

For poems by Theodore Roethke, to Faber and Faber Ltd., from *The Far Field*, and to Martin Secker & Warburg Limited from *Words for the Wind*.

For poems by E. A. Robinson: 'The Poor Relation', 'Eros Turannos' and 'Hillcrest', reprinted with permission of The Macmillan Company from *Collected Poems* by Edwin Arlington Robinson, Copyright 1916 by Edwin Arlington Robinson, renewed 1944 by Ruth Nivision. 'Luke Havergal' is reprinted with the permission of Charles Scribner's Sons from *The Children of the Night* by Edwin Arlington Robinson.

For poems by Duncan Campbell Scott, reprinted by permission of the Canadian Publishers, McClelland and Stewart Limited, Toronto.

For poems by Wallace Stevens, to Faber and Faber, Ltd.

For poems by F. R. Scott, to the author.

ACKNOWLEDGEMENTS

For a poem by Allen Tate, from *Poems 1920–45*, to Eyre and Spottiswoode, Ltd.

For poems by Richard Wilbur, to Faber and Faber, Ltd.

For poems by William Carlos Williams, to MacGibbon and Kee, Ltd.

Contents

CONTENTS

Introduction

I

American poets are strange: Emily Dickinson in her solitary room, Walt Whitman the bearded nurse, Wallace Stevens at the insurance office, Edgar Allen Poe the necrophiliac Southern gentleman. When an American writes a poem, he commits an unAmerican activity. He takes a step to the side, away from the centre. No American writer of any value feels that he represents his country. Though many of the best writers anywhere are eccentric, in other countries there are always a few who speak for the national spirit. In the United States it is Longfellow who tries to be the central figure, and Longfellow is third-rate. Instead of a city that serves as a centre of wit and imagination, we have the provincial professionalism of the academies. The closest thing to a café in New York is Columbia University. Instead of the man of Letters in his intellectual Paris, radiating poems back to the provinces, we have Hart Crane of Akron, Ohio, who writes ecstatic homosexual love poems, attempts an epic, knocks around New York, gets himself deported from France, and kills himself by jumping off a ship into the Gulf of Mexico.

The eccentricity of American poetry is not to be praised nor blamed—nor need it be as brutal as Crane's: Herman Melville's withdrawal was quiet; Whitman's eccentricities were kindly. But middle-class life and poetry have proved irreconcilable, and America has not yet found (or required) a social antithesis to the middle-class —a community of intellectuals and artists. The forms and mystiques of American poetry have been a series of unique inventions, with little continuity or growth. As you look through the poems in this anthology, many of the early ones (and some of the later ones too) would be perfectly at ease in the Oxford Book of English Verse; some of them are good—but they are not the very best. When they stop looking English, they start to be great poems. I am not speaking of superficialities of content ('The Indian Burial Ground') or of dialect, but of the real spiritual originality of a Walt Whitman.

The history of English poetry was a burden to American poets. There was one language to write in, and that language happened to own the greatest body of lyric poetry in the world. What could Longfellow do, but be a homespun Tennyson? A few poets had different ideas: eccentricity—formal and spiritual—was an escape from Englishness. It was one way out, only it had to be resolute and thorough; there was no picking up of other people's tricks, no community. The only way out of Englishness lay in an unrelenting plunge into the unique self. Louis Simpson has written an accurate little poem called, 'American Poetry':

> Whatever it is, it must have
> A stomach that can digest
> Rubber, coal, uranium, moons, poems.
>
> Like the shark, it contains a shoe
> It must swim for miles through the desert
> Uttering cries that are almost human.

It is hard to remember the burden of Englishness. Now American poets are confident of the greatness of American poetry. The uneasy deference to English poetry, a hundred years ago, has changed to an easy scorn of recent English poetry, a scorn that is seldom based on familiarity. The old poets are admired but felt to be useless. A new collection of primitive poetry (Esquimaux, African, Melanesian) is more likely to influence young American poets than John Donne is. Out of this state of confident eclecticism, it is possible that a community of artists may grow.

2

Here is an anthology of American poetry which does not include 'Song of Myself,' 'Paterson,' 'The Bridge,' or 'The Cantos.' Actually no anthology includes them, because they are too long, and thus no anthology is representative, since a good portion of the greatness of American poetry resides in these longer poems. I have chosen to represent Whitman, Williams, Crane and Pound by the best of their shorter poems. The reader who admires a particular poet will follow him further in the library.

As this small anthology can only suggest the range of American poetry, so this introduction cannot be more than a hint of a hint. My opening generalizations largely preclude further generalization: we are dealing with a group of people distinguished by their differences from each other. I think that my best course of action is not to try to make statements to which there must be massive exceptions, nor to run through a list of poets and make a tiny summary of each —I do a bit of this in my biographical notes—but to write about a few of them at slightly greater length. Because they are various and therefore representative, I will write small introductions to Walt Whitman, Emily Dickinson, Robert Frost, Ezra Pound, Wallace Stevens and Theodore Roethke.

3

Walt Whitman was born on Long Island in 1819, son of a small farmer who moved to Brooklyn and became a carpenter. Whitman attended school briefly, became a printer, a country schoolteacher and an editor of contentious political newspapers. He wrote propaganda and sentimental fiction for a number of years, and suddenly in his thirties began to write the enormously original poems of *Leaves of Grass,* of which the first edition appeared in 1855. During the Civil War he acted as a male nurse among the wounded of both sides in the vicinity of Washington. After the war he lived largely in Brooklyn until his death in 1892, leading a quiet and semi-invalid life, writing new poems and publishing enlarged editions of *Leaves of Grass.* In his lifetime, his poetry was considered shocking and went largely unread.

Because Whitman wrote frequently about America and about democracy, he has been considered a national poet, and a poet of the outsides of things. Occasionally he achieved the banality of nationalism, but for the most part his America is a dreamed and inward continent, as much internal as his 'Passage to India' through 'the seas of God.' In his great 'Song of Myself,' he is everyman, like Joyce's *Ulysses.* He appears amid the New England poets of the 19th century (Longfellow, Lowell, Emerson, Whittier) like a creature from another planet. In a sense, he is. With the exception of the

Quaker Whittier, the others are all University Wits, Brahmins who looked to English poetry for sources and to the English public for approval. Whitman was Himself, a condition that he called 'America.'

'Out of the Cradle Endlessly Rocking' and 'When Lilacs Last in the Dooryard Bloom'd,' both poems of universal mourning (though the second uses the death of President Lincoln as an occasion) are his finest shorter works. Mourning is perhaps Whitman's tenderest and deepest source of feeling. In the first of these poems Whitman addresses a bird that has lost its mate:

Yes my brother I know,
The rest might not, but I have treasur'd every note,
For more than once dimly down to the beach gliding,
Silent, avoiding the moonbeams, blending myself with the shadows,
Recalling now the obscure shapes, the echoes, the sounds and sights
    after their sorts,
The white arms out in the breakers tirelessly tossing,
I, with bare feet, a child, the wind wafting my hair,
Listen'd long and long.

There are poems out of the war, animal poems that remind the reader of D. H. Lawrence's indebtedness to Whitman, and tiny imagist fragments that might have been written by an American in London in 1912. Reading through a comprehensive selection of Whitman, one is constantly astonished at the range, intensity and originality of America's greatest poet. And one will never solve the mystery of this solitary, unbegotten genius.

4

Emily Dickinson is nearly as strange as Whitman, but she is eccentric where he is mysterious. She lived her entire life (1830–1886) in her father's house in Amherst, Massachusetts. At the beginning of her intensely private life, she seems to have desired literary fame, but when her unique poems—with their hymn-tune rhythms, off-rhymes, and extreme metaphors—did not please the conventional taste of contemporary editors, she withdrew from literary conten-

tion, and in fact only published in her lifetime three of the two
thousand poems she wrote. After her death her literary vicissitudes
continued, as her editors re-wrote her poems and made them more
ordinary and more acceptable to popular taste. It was not until 1958
that her work became available in an accurate text.

In the great volume of her work, there is much that is whimsical
and flimsy, but there are many poems of a strong and original
power. Writing it seems for herself only, she punctuates largely
with dashes, and writes so personally that she remains reticent.

> I cannot live with You—
> It would be Life—
> And Life is over there—
> Behind the Shelf
>
> The Sexton keeps the Key to—
> Putting up
> Our Life—His Porcelain—
> Like a Cup—
>
> Discarded of the Housewife—
> Quaint—or Broke—
> A newer Sevres pleases—
> Old Ones crack—
>
> I could not die—with You—
> For One must wait
> To shut the Other's Gaze down—
> You—could not—

She is writing about a lover whom she is unable to marry, or to live
with, or to keep. We have small idea of his identity, or even of his
reality. The poem ends:

> So We must meet apart—
> You there—I—here—
> With just the Door ajar
> That Oceans are—and Prayer—
> And that White Sustenance—
> Despair—

The last two lines are the quintessence of Emily Dickinson. It is typical that her early editors, unable to accept the harshness of 'white,' substituted the poetically acceptable 'pale.'

5

Robert Frost was born in California but moved to New England when he was a boy, grew up in Massachusetts, and associated himself with the region in his writing. He attended Dartmouth College and Harvard as a young man, but was graduated from neither. He married young, settled on a farm and lived for many years on a small stipend from his grandfather. He farmed little, and wrote without success. Later he taught school for several years, and then in 1912 took his family to England, where he lived among the Georgian poets, and became a close friend of Edward Thomas. It was in England that Frost published his first two books of poems; English poets, publishers and reviewers were the first to recognize his ability. When he returned to the United States in 1915, the beginnings of his fame preceded him. He made his living largely by lecturing and informal teaching—he was Poet in Residence at Michigan, Amherst and Dartmouth—and became enormously popular in his own lifetime. He won the Pulitzer Prize three times, and was celebrated everywhere as a national poet.

The figure that was celebrated, and the real man, were widely dissimilar. When Frost went to England he liked to pass himself off, with at least some of his new acquaintances, as a simple farmer, a peasant poet. When critics repeated this invention in print, he was furious. But he created the myth himself. He was an urbane and sophisticated man, who read Latin poets for recreation and who was quick with an epigram. Sometimes on the lecture platform, even late in his life, he would play the rural part to delight the cooing old ladies in front of him. Afterwards he would sip a martini among the professors and make wicked insinuations about those critics he considered his enemies.

The poetry is another thing. American magazines gave the impression that Frost was a benign master of common sense and folk wisdom. Many of his admirers have gone to considerable trouble to

misunderstand him. In 'Mending Wall' Frost ridicules a neighbour
who says, 'Good fences make good neighbours' (and tries to turn
alienation into companionship). Yet Stewart Udall, Secretary of the
Interior under Presidents Kennedy and Johnson, and a great sup-
porter of Robert Frost, has quoted the line as Frost's own sentiment.
So have others. The real Frost is romantic, alienated, egocentric,
suicidal and frequently as dark as the rest of dark American literature.
The best of Frost is the black Frost, as in 'Design':

> I found a dimpled spider, fat and white,
> On a white heal-all, holding up a moth
> Like a white piece of rigid satin cloth—
> Assorted characters of death and blight
> Mixed ready to begin the morning right,
> Like the ingredients of a witches' broth—
> A snow-drop spider, a flower like froth,
> And dead wings carried like a paper kite.
>
> What had that flower to do with being white,
> The wayside blue and innocent heal-all?
> What brought the kindred spider to that height,
> Then steered the white moth thither in the night?
> What but design of darkness to appall?—
> If design govern in a thing so small.

At first the worst evil seems to be evil purpose, and then Frost lets
us see that purposelessness is more terrifying still.

There are fine lyrics like 'The Pasture' in which there is nothing of
darkness at all. There are other poems in which the darkness is
kidded, evaded and made small. These bad poems attempt to serve a
psychic purpose; Frost described poems as occupational therapy,
like those bracelets and wallets which psychiatrists have madmen
make, as a means toward form and control. His best poems, one
suspects, were psychically more successful. Frequently, he deals
with his fear of madness or his longing for oblivion: 'The woods
are lovely, dark and deep.' In many of his best poems, Frost was *not*
reconciled to age and death, or at least he dealt with feelings of
being unreconciled, as in 'Out, out—,' in which a young boy dies
after a foolish accident, 'And they, since they/Were not the one dead,

B

turned to their affairs.' His greatest poem of ageing is 'To Earthward,' which begins with images of love in youth:

> Love at the lips was touch
> As sweet as I could bear;
>
> . . .
>
> I had the swirl and ache
> From sprays of honeysuckle
> That when they're gathered shake
> Dew on the knuckle.

And ends with a loss of feeling which leads into the lightly disguised desire to die:

> When stiff and sore and scarred
> I take away my hand
> From leaning on it hard
> In grass and sand,
>
> The hurt is not enough:
> I long for weight and strength
> To feel the earth as rough
> To all my length.

A problem that vexed him all his life was the ego's thick walls. He found himself frequently isolated within himself and by himself. 'He thought he kept the universe alone,' as he wrote in 'The Most of It,'

> And nothing ever came of what he cried
> Unless it was the embodiment that crashed
> In the cliff's talus on the other side,
> And then in the far distant water splashed,
> But after a time allowed for it to swim,
> Instead of proving human when it neared
> And someone else additional to him,
> As a great buck it powerfully appeared,
> Pushing the crumpled water up ahead,
> And landed pouring like a waterfall,
> And stumbled through the rocks with horny tread,
> And forced the underbrush—and that was all.

A thoroughly professional poet, dedicated to the promotion of his career and reputation, he was a serious and desperate questioner of the 'trial by existence,' a public fraud, and privately a great poet.

6

Wallace Stevens is another poet who is constantly known by a sort of tag-line. As Pound is 'the Fascist,' Stevens is 'the insurance man.' In keeping with the series of incongruities that compose the history of American poetry, he was an insurance man who wrote delicate symbolist poems, more rarified and obscure than the writing of his poetic contemporaries who made their living in a more literary fashion. He was born in Pennsylvania in 1879, and died in Connecticut in 1955. When he was a young man at Harvard he wrote verses like these:

> Ah yes! beyond these barren walls
>   Two hearts shall in a garden meet,
> And while the latest robin calls,
>   Her lips to his shall be made sweet.

> And out above these gloomy tow'rs
>   The full moon tenderly shall rise
> To cast its light upon the flow'rs,
>   And find him looking in her eyes.

For a twenty-one-year-old undergraduate in the United States in 1900, these lines are predictable and perhaps slightly better than predictable. If one examines the *Atlantic Monthly* for the same period, one finds little that is better. (E. A. Robinson and Robert Frost were writing well, but no one knew it.)

Stevens went to law school after he was graduated from Harvard, and in 1904 was admitted to the Bar in New York. He lived in the City for a time, and associated with the group of poets who were not expatriates, and who tended to congregate in Greenwich Village: Alfred Kreymbourg, Marianne Moore, William Carlos Williams. This part of Stevens' life tends to be forgotten by critics who wish to emphasize his separation from the literary world. He began to publish the first poems that go into *Harmonium* ten years before that book appeared in 1923. In 1916 he took a job in the legal department of Hartford Accident and Indemnity. In 1934 he became vice-president. His position required him to live in Hartford, and it was there that he spent the rest of his life—by day a vice-president, by night the author of:

> It was her voice that made
> The sky acutest at its vanishing.
> She measured to the hour its solitude.
> She was the single artificer of the world
> In which she sang. And when she sang, the sea,
> Whatever self it had, became the self
> That was her song, for she was the maker. . .

The poems of *Harmonium* are still the best known, especially the superb 'Sunday Morning' with its highly accomplished blank verse. (Stevens is the only poet to have written with exquisite technique both free and metered verse.) Some of the earliest poems have an expressive distortion to them, and remind us of some of the most recent American poets:

Disillusionment of Ten O'Clock

> The houses are haunted
> By white night-gowns.
> None are green,
> Or purple with green rings,
> Or green with yellow rings,
> Or yellow with blue rings.
> None of them are strange,
> With socks of lace
> And beaded ceintures.
> People are not going
> To dream of baboons and periwinkles.
> Only, here and there, an old sailor,
> Drunk and asleep in his boots,
> Catches tigers
> In red weather.

But for the most part Stevens is a philosophical symbolist, ruminating over the themes of aesthetic nihilism, imagination and reality.

A gap of thirteen years separated *Harmonium* from its successor, *Ideas of Order* (1936), and for many readers there was a gap of quality too. The gorgeousness of much of *Harmonium* was followed by a certain dryness. Certainly there was a period of little poetry (which Stevens compensated for at the end of his life with another time of great fecundity—the period of *The Auroras of Autumn*, *The Rock*, and *An Ordinary Evening in New Haven*) but looked at in retrospect, there is a remarkable consistency in the quality of Stevens' poetry. It changes (and no one ever likes to see an admired poet change; it always seems for the worse) but it does not decline. At the end of his life, living his rather isolated life of retirement in Hartford, he could still write a poem like this one:

The Course of a Particular

Today the leaves cry, hanging on branches swept by wind,
Yet the nothingness of winter becomes a little less.
It is still full of icy shades and shapen snow.

The leaves cry . . . One holds off and merely hears the cry.
It is a busy cry, concerning someone else.
And though one says that one is part of everything,

There is a conflict, there is a resistance involved;
And being part is an exertion that declines:
One feels the life of that which gives life as it is.

The leaves cry. It is not a cry of divine attention,
Nor the smoke-drift of puffed-out heroes, nor human cry.
It is the cry of leaves that do not transcend themselves,

In the absence of fantasia, without meaning more
Than they are in the final finding of the air, in the thing
Itself, until, at last, the cry concerns no one at all.

7

Ezra Pound was born in Hailey, Idaho, but was brought back East as an infant. He grew up in the suburbs of Philadelphia, where his father was employed at the mint. He attended the University of

Pennsylvania and Haverford College as an undergraduate, and began work on his Ph.D. at the University of Pennsylvania. Fellow students were William Carlos Williams and Hilda Doolittle, or H.D. He was a bright, academic student, with particular interests in romance literature and in writing poems. He had visited Europe and enjoyed it, but perhaps he would have become an American professor had his first academic job worked out. He was fired by Wabash College in Crawfordsville, Indiana, after giving shelter for the night, in his rooming house run by spinster sisters, to a dancing girl who had been abandoned by her troupe. For the rest of his life he has been a professor manqué, grandly teaching and aiding the young, while from his various perches in expatriate Europe he denounced the culture of America and its universities. He also became a great poet, and by far the most efficient propagandist of good new writing.

The men he discovered or promoted at the start of their careers include T. S. Eliot, James Joyce, Ernest Hemingway and Robert Frost. (One could go on and on with lesser names, and seldom find a mistake.) His recognition of Frost—an older man writing in an alien tradition—shows how sure and flexible was his taste: he saw genius in both the unknown authors of 'The Love Song of J. Alfred Prufrock,' and 'The Death of the Hired Man.' When he met Eliot and Frost, he lived in London, where he had come to listen to Ford Madox Ford and William Butler Yeats, for whom he sometimes served as secretary. In the twenties he went to Paris, and a few years later to Italy, where he lived in Rapallo writing *The Cantos* and became increasingly absorbed in his study of economics and in the promulgation of Social Credit. His respect for authoritarianism led him to an admiration for Mussolini, and during the second world war he broadcast to America from Italy by short wave. After the war he was judged mentally unfit to stand trial for treason, and spent many years under guard at St. Elizabeth's Hospital in Washington, D.C. In 1958, he was freed in the custody of his wife and returned to Italy.

His earliest published poetry is largely appalling. It consists of mawkish archaic imitations of romance poetry; it is like graduate student verse:

Lord God of Heaven that with mercy dight
Th'alternate prayer wheel of the night and light
Eternal hath to thee, and in whose sight
Our days as rain drops in the sea surge fall, . . .

but it is not merely graduate student verse: there is a certain *extremity*
to it. The way in which it is appalling is almost promising; it is so
bad it is original.

Pound's taste for pastiche led him to Browning, whose conversa-
tional tone was relatively modern; and his good taste itself led him
to Yeats. He was as gregarious and literary, in his young years, as
Frost was solitary and withdrawn. In London he met T. E. Hulme,
that fountain of half-articulated ideas, and appropriated and
extended Hulme's idea of the image into Imagism. 'In a Station of
the Metro' is one of the results. This devotion to the pictorial image
led him to Oriental poetry; one of Pound's greatest contributions to
modern literature has been his invention of Chinese poetry for our
time and our language. Aided by the notes of a late sinologist,
Ernest Fenollosa, Pound wrote about the Chinese character as a
compressed image, and made English poems like 'The River
Merchant's Wife' out of raw translations. The simplicity, even
starkness, of these translations, was an antidote to Pound's romance
floridity. Still, his verse had lacked content; he had, like Browning,
assumed a series of personae, and had developed character; then he
had turned to the accurate representation of the world outside. It
was the Great War which turned him to thoughts about society, and
had its particular monument in Pound's 'Mauberly.' The ear and
the eye of the master are here, and the compassion is added:

Daring as never before, wastage as never before,
Young blood and high blood,
fair cheeks, and fine bodies;

fortitude as never before

frankness as never before,
disillusions as never told in the old days,
hysterias, trench confessions,
laughter out of dead bellies.

[23]

A little later Pound began to publish *The Cantos*, his bringing-up-to-date of Dante. Huge, paranoid, compassionate, obscure, the *Cantos* are a great poem in spite of themselves, another in the history of American mad masterpieces like *Moby Dick* and 'Song of Myself.' His poems, his literary discoveries and his critical influence place him as the central figure (which is not to say the greatest artist) within modern American poetry; it is paradoxical, but typical of the national literature, that this central figure lived most of his life in Europe and was accused of treason to the United States.

8

Theodore Roethke was born in Saginaw, Michigan, in 1908, son of a Prussian florist. He died in 1963 in the State of Washington, where he taught at the University of Washington in Seattle. His life was superficially like the life of many of his contemporaries—teaching, poetry readings, the usual prizes—but the resemblance is only on the outside. Roethke was afflicted with a mental illness which forced him to enter hospitals frequently in his adult life. He would remain in the hospital for a month or two, and then return to the world and to his teaching. The continual battle with madness marked his poetry.

His earliest work, in *Open House* (1941), is tightly metered and rhymed, and highly rational. The verse is a cage for the beast of madness. By 1947, when he published *The Lost Son*, he was able to court the irrational. His memory of his father's greenhouse was always central to him, and he became a poet of negative capability:

> I can hear, underground, that sucking and sobbing,
> In my veins, in my bones I feel it,—
> The small waters seeping upward,
> The tight grains parting at last.
> When sprouts break out,
> Slippery as fish,
> I quail, lean to beginnings, sheath-wet.

'The Lost Son' itself was part of a long autobiographical sequence which was finished in *Praise to the End* (1951) and which inhabited largely the world of dream and nightmare.

The other side, the more rational and technical side of the man, wrote many poems in tight end-stopped pentameters, some of them blighted by too close a resemblance to Yeats, but others succeeding by their very delight in metered speech:

> I knew a woman, lovely in her bones,
> When small birds sighed, she would sigh back at them;
> Ah, when she moved, she moved more ways than one:
> The shapes a bright container can contain!
> Of her choice virtues only gods should speak,
> Or English poets who grew up on Greek
> (I'd have them sing in chorus, cheek to cheek).

Still, it was the romantic and irrational self that wrote the greatest poems. Toward the end of his life, he made poems in a style that was far from dream (sometimes in the autobiographical sequence we feel that dream is disguise) but which entered new territories and depths of feeling. I am thinking of poems like 'The Rose' and of lines like these:

> Near this rose, in this grove of sun-parched, wind-warped
> madronas,
> Among the half-dead trees, I came upon the true ease of
> myself,
> As if another man appeared out of the depths of my being,
> And I stood outside myself,
> Beyond becoming and perishing,
> A something wholly other,
> As if I swayed out on the wildest wave alive,
> And yet was still.
> And I rejoiced in being what I was:
> In the lilac change, the white reptilian calm,
> In the bird beyond the bough, the single one
> With all the air to greet him as he flies,
> The dolphin rising from the darkening waves;
>
> And in this rose, this rose in the sea-wind,
> Rooted in stone, keeping the whole of light,
> Gathering to itself sound and silence—
> Mine and the sea-wind's.

This book is a compromise between a representation of what has happened in American poetry (Freneau, Longfellow, Whittier) and a collection of the best (Dickinson, Whitman). On the other hand, I have tried to include the best of a minor figure rather than the most representative. A patch of *Hiawatha* might have its historical interest, but 'The Jewish Cemetery at Newport' is better verse. In a book of this size, I have found it necessary to exclude certain minimal figures like James Russell Lowell and Oliver Wendell Holmes, and in the pursuit of fidelity to the best of poetry, I have found that modern poetry dominates the book. I have stopped with Richard Wilbur (b. 1921) because of the size and nature of this book. For those who wish to read poetry by younger Americans, I suggest my Penguin *Contemporary American Poets*.

I have included several Canadian poets, who are identified in the biographical notes, in order to make this a book of North American verse, and not only of the United States.

D.H.
February 1, 1967

Anne Bradstreet

1612?–1672

Daughter and wife to two of the first governors of the Massachusetts Bay Colony, Anne Bradstreet was born in England and became the first acknowledged poet of North America. Her *The Tenth Muse Lately Sprung up in America* appeared in England in 1650.

A Letter to her Husband, Absent upon Publick Employment

As loving Hind that (Hartless) wants her Deer,
Scuds through the woods and fern with harkning ear,
Perplext, in every bush & nook doth pry
Her dearest Deer might answer ear or eye:
So doth my anxious soul, which now doth miss
A dearer Dear (far dearer Heart) than this,
Still wait with doubts, & hopes, and failing eye,
His voice to hear or person to discry.
Or as the pensive Dove doth all alone
On withered bough most uncouthly bemoan
The absence of her Love and loving Mate,
Whose loss hath made her so unfortunate:
Ev'n thus doe I, with many a deep sad groan,
Bewail my turtle true, who now is gone,
His presence and his safe return still woo
With thousand dolefull sighs & mournfull Coo.
Or as the loving Mullet that true Fish,
Her fellow lost, nor joy nor life doth wish,
But lanches on that shore there for to dye
Where she her captive husband doth espy.
Mine being gone, I lead a joyless life,
I have a loving fere, yet seem no wife:
But worst of all, to him can't steer my course,
I here, he there, alas, both kept by force.
Return my Dear, my joy, my only Love,
Unto thy Hinde, thy Mullet and thy Dove,

Who neither joyes in pasture, house nor streams;
The substance gone, O me, these are but dreams.
Together at one Tree, oh let us brouze,
And like two Turtles roost within one house,
And like the Mullets in one River glide,
Let's still remain but one, till death divide.
      Thy loving Love and Dearest Dear,
      At home, abroad, and every where,

                        A.B.

Edward Taylor

1645?–1729

Unpublished until 1939, Edward Taylor is the best Colonial poet.
He emigrated in 1668, was graduated from Harvard, and practised
medicine and divinity in Westfield, Massachusetts.

Upon a Spider Catching a Fly

Thou sorrow, venom Elfe:
  Is this thy play,
To spin a web out of thyselfe
  To Catch a Fly?
    For why?

I saw a pettish wasp
  Fall foule therein:
Whom yet thy whorle pins did not hasp
  Lest he should fling
    His sting.

But as afraid, remote
  Didst stand hereat,
And with thy little fingers stroke
  And gently tap
    His back.

Thus gently him didst treate
  Lest he should pet,
And in a froppish, aspish heate
  Should greatly fret
    Thy net.

Whereas the silly Fly,
  Caught by its leg,
Thou by the throate took'st hastily,
  And 'hinde the head
    Bite Dead.

This goes to pot, that not
  Nature doth call.
Strive not above what strength hath got,
  Lest in the brawle
    Thou fall.

This Fray seems thus to us:
  Hells Spider gets
His intrails spun to whip Cords thus,
  And wove to nets,
    And sets.

To tangle Adams race
  In's stratagems
To their Destructions, Spoil'd, made base
  By venom things,
    Damn'd Sins.

But mighty, Gracious Lord,
  Communicate
Thy Grace to breake the Cord; afford
  Us Glorys Gate
    And State.

We'll Nightingaile sing like,
  When pearcht on high
In Glories Cage, thy glory, bright:
  Yea, thankfully,
    For joy.

Huswifery

Make me, O Lord, thy Spinning Wheele compleat;
  Thy Holy Worde my Distaff make for mee.
Make mine Affections thy Swift Flyers neate,
  And make my Soule thy holy Spoole to bee.
  My Conversation make to be thy Reele,
  And reele the yarn thereon spun of thy Wheele.

Make me thy Loome then, knit therein this Twine:
  And make thy Holy Spirit, Lord, winde quills:
Then weave the Web thyselfe. The yarn is fine.
  Thine Ordinances make my Fulling Mills.
  Then dye the same in Heavenly Colours Choice,
  All pinkt with Varnish't flowers of Paradise.

Then cloath therewith mine Understanding, Will,
  Affections, Judgment, Conscience, Memory;
My Words and Actions, that their shine may fill
  My wayes with glory and thee glorify.
  Then mine apparell shall display before yee
  That I am Cloathd in Holy robes for glory.

Philip Freneau
1752–1832

Freneau was a revolutionary, a sea-captain, a journalist and a politician. His nationalism was fanatic, and yet his verses remained tied to the traditions of English poetry.

The Indian Burying Ground

In spite of all the learned have said,
 I still my old opinion keep;
The posture, that we give the dead,
 Points out the soul's eternal sleep.

Not so the ancients of these lands—
 The Indian, when from life released,
Again is seated with his friends,
 And shares again the joyous feast.

His imaged birds, and painted bowl,
 And venison, for a journey dressed,
Bespeak the nature of the soul,
 Activity, that knows no rest.

His bow, for action ready bent,
 And arrows, with a head of stone,
Can only mean that life is spent,
 And not the old ideas gone.

Thou, stranger, that shalt come this way,
 No fraud upon the dead commit—
Observe the swelling turf, and say
 They do not lie, but here they sit.

Here still a lofty rock remains,
 On which the curious eye may trace
(Now wasted, half, by wearing rains)
 The fancies of a ruder race.

Here still an aged elm aspires,
  Beneath whose far-projecting shade
(And which the shepherd still admires)
  The children of the forest played!

There oft a restless Indian queen
  (Pale Shebah, with her braided hair)
And many a barbarous form is seen
  To chide the man that lingers there.

By midnight moons, o'er moistening dews;
  In habit for the chase arrayed,
The hunter still the deer pursues,
  The hunter and the deer, a shade!

And long shall timorous fancy see
  The painted chief, and pointed spear,
And Reason's self shall bow the knee
  To shadows and delusions here.

William Cullen Bryant
1794–1878

Bryant's poems were chiefly written in his youth. In later life he
turned to journalism and politics, and became a leading figure in
New York City. *Thanatopsis* was written when he was seventeen
and revised when he was twenty-seven; it remains his best poem.

Thanatopsis

To him who in the love of Nature holds
Communion with her visible forms, she speaks
A various language; for his gayer hours
She has a voice of gladness, and a smile
And eloquence of beauty, and she glides
Into his darker musings, with a mild
And healing sympathy, that steals away
Their sharpness, ere he is aware. When thoughts
Of the last bitter hour come like a blight
Over thy spirit, and sad images
Of the stern agony, and shroud, and pall,
And breathless darkness, and the narrow house,
Make thee to shudder, and grow sick at heart;—
Go forth, under the open sky, and list
To Nature's teachings, while from all around—
Earth and her waters, and the depths of air—
Comes a still voice—Yet a few days, and thee
The all-beholding sun shall see no more
In all his course; nor yet in the cold ground,
Where thy pale form was laid, with many tears,
Nor in the embrace of ocean, shall exist
Thy image. Earth, that nourished thee, shall claim
Thy growth, to be resolved to earth again,
And, lost each human trace, surrendering up
Thine individual being, shalt thou go
To mix for ever with the elements,
To be a brother to the insensible rock
And to the sluggish clod, which the rude swain

[34]

Turns with his share, and treads upon. The oak
Shall send his roots abroad, and pierce thy mould.

Yet not to thine eternal resting-place
Shalt thou retire alone, nor couldst thou wish
Couch more magnificent. Thou shalt lie down
With patriarchs of the infant world—with kings,
The powerful of the earth—the wise, the good,
Fair forms, and hoary seers of ages past,
All in one mighty sepulchre. The hills
Rock-ribbed and ancient as the sun,—the vales
Stretching in pensive quietness between;
The venerable woods—rivers that move
In majesty, and the complaining brooks
That make the meadows green; and, poured round all,
Old Ocean's gray and melancholy waste,—
Are but the solemn decorations all
Of the great tomb of man. The golden sun,
The planets, all the infinite host of heaven,
Are shining on the sad abodes of death,
Through the still lapse of ages. All that tread
The globe are but a handful to the tribes
That slumber in its bosom.—Take the wings
Of morning, pierce the Barcan wilderness,
Or lose thyself in the continuous woods
Where rolls the Oregon, and hears no sound,
Save his own dashings—yet the dead are there:
And millions in those solitudes, since first
The flight of years began, have laid them down
In their last sleep—the dead reign there alone.
So shalt thou rest, and what if thou withdraw
In silence from the living, and no friend
Take note of thy departure? All that breathe
Will share thy destiny. The gay will laugh
When thou art gone, the solemn brood of care
Plod on, and each one as before will chase
His favourite phantom; yet all these shall leave
Their mirth and their employments, and shall come
And make their bed with thee. As the long train
Of ages glide away, the sons of men,

The youth in life's green spring, and he who goes
In the full strength of years, matron and maid,
The speechless babe, and the gray-headed man—
Shall one by one be gathered to thy side,
By those, who in their turn shall follow them.

So live, that when thy summons comes to join
The innumerable caravan, which moves
To that mysterious realm, where each shall take
His chamber in the silent halls of death,
Thou go not, like the quarry-slave at night,
Scourged to his dungeon, but, sustained and soothed
But an unfaltering trust, approach thy grave,
Like one who wraps the drapery of his couch
About him, and lies down to pleasant dreams.

Ralph Waldo Emerson

1803–1882

Emerson was the most celebrated American philosopher of his day, and nearly as famous in England as in the United States. Lecturer, essayist and Unitarian minister, he included the writing of poetry among his many talents. To his credit is his early recognition of the genius of Walt Whitman, despite the relative conservatism of Emerson's literary forms and personal morality.

Concord Hymn

Sung at the completion of the Battle Monument, July 4, 1837

By the rude bridge that arched the flood,
   Their flag to April's breeze unfurled,
Here once the embattled farmers stood
   And fired the shot heard round the world.

The foe long since in silence slept;
   Alike the conqueror silent sleeps;
And Time the ruined bridge has swept
   Down the dark stream which seaward creeps.

On this green bank, by this soft stream,
   We set to-day a votive stone;
That memory may their deed redeem,
   When, like our sires, our sons are gone.

Spirit, that made those heroes dare
   To die, and leave their children free,
Bid Time and Nature gently spare
   The shaft we raise to them and thee.

Days

Daughters of Time, the hypocritic Days,
Muffled and dumb like barefoot dervishes,

And marching single in an endless file,
Bring diadems and fagots in their hands.
To each they offer gifts after his will,
Bread, kingdoms, stars, and sky that hold them all.
I, in my pleached garden, watched the pomp,
Forgot my morning wishes, hastily
Took a few herbs and apples, and the Day
Turned and departed silent. I, too late,
Under her solemn fillet saw the scorn.

Brahma

If the red slayer think he slays,
  Or if the slain think he is slain,
They know not well the subtle ways
  I keep, and pass, and turn again.

Far or forgot to me is near;
  Shadow and sunlight are the same;
The vanished gods to me appear;
  And one to me are shame and fame.

They reckon ill who leave me out;
  When me they fly, I am the wings;
I am the doubter and the doubt,
  And I the hymn the Brahmin sings.

The strong gods pine for my abode,
  And pine in vain the sacred Seven;
But thou, meek lover of the good!
  Find me, and turn thy back on heaven.

Henry Wadsworth Longfellow
1807–1882

Professor at Harvard and would-be writer of national epics, Long-
fellow is the prototype of the Brahmin who continues as one version
of the American poet. His strained and pathetic narrative poems go
unread, yet there is a pleasant meditative lyrical strain in some of his
odes and sonnets.

The Jewish Cemetery at Newport

How strange it seems! These Hebrews in their graves,
   Close by the street of this fair seaport town,
Silent beside the never-silent waves,
   At rest in all this moving up and down!

The trees are white with dust, that o'er their sleep
   Wave their broad curtains in the southwind's breath,
While underneath these leafy tents they keep
   The long, mysterious Exodus of Death.

And these sepulchral stones, so old and brown,
   That pave with level flags their burial-place,
Seem like the tablets of the Law, thrown down
   And broken by Moses at the mountain's base.

The very names recorded here are strange,
   Of foreign accent, and of different climes;
Alvares and Rivera interchange
   With Abraham and Jacob of old times.

'Blessed be God, for he created Death!'
   The mourners said, 'and Death is rest and peace';
Then added, in the certainty of faith,
   'And giveth Life that nevermore shall cease.'

Closed are the portals of their Synagogue,
   No Psalms of David now the silence break,
No Rabbi reads the ancient Decalogue
   In the grand dialect the Prophets spake.

[39]

Gone are the living, but the dead remain,
  And not neglected; for a hand unseen,
Scattering its bounty, like a summer rain,
  Still keeps their graves and their remembrance green.

How came they here? What burst of Christian hate,
  What persecution, merciless and blind,
Drove o'er the sea—that desert desolate—
  These Ishmaels and Hagars of mankind?

They lived in narrow streets and lanes obscure,
  Ghetto and Judenstrass, in mirk and mire;
Taught in the school of patience to endure
  The life of anguish and the death of fire.

All their lives long, with the unleavened bread
  And bitter herbs of exile and its fears,
The wasting famine of the heart they fed,
  And slaked its thirst with marah of their tears.

Anathema maranatha! was the cry
  That rang from town to town, from street to street:
At every gate the accursed Mordecai
  Was mocked and jeered, and spurned by Christian feet.

Pride and humiliation hand in hand
  Walked with them through the world where'er they went;
Trampled and beaten were they as the sand,
  And yet unshaken as the continent.

For in the background figures vague and vast
  Of patriarchs and of prophets rose sublime,
And all the great traditions of the Past
  They saw reflected in the coming time.

And thus forever with reverted look
  The mystic volume of the world they read,
Spelling it backward, like a Hebrew book,
  Till life became a Legend of the Dead.

But ah! what once has been shall be no more!
　　The groaning earth in travail and in pain
Brings forth its races, but does not restore,
　　And the dead nations never rise again.

Divina Commedia

Oft have I seen at some cathedral door
　　A labourer, pausing in the dust and heat,
　　Lay down his burden, and with reverent feet
Enter, and cross himself, and on the floor
Kneel to repeat his paternoster o'er;
　　Far off the noises of the world retreat;
　　The loud vociferations of the street
Become an undistinguishable roar.
So, as I enter here from day to day,
　　And leave my burden at this minster gate,
　　Kneeling in prayer, and not ashamed to pray,
The tumult of the time disconsolate
　　To inarticulate murmurs dies away,
　　While the eternal ages watch and wait.

Chaucer

An old man in a lodge within a park;
　　The chamber walls depicted all around
　　With portraitures of huntsman, hawk, and hound,
　　And the hurt deer. He listeneth to the lark,
Whose song comes with the sunshine through the dark
　　Of painted glass in leaden lattice bound;
　　He listeneth and he laugheth at the sound,
　　Then writeth in a book like any clerk.
He is the poet of the dawn, who wrote
　　The Canterbury Tales, and his old age
　　Made beautiful with song; and as I read
I hear the crowing cock, I hear the note
　　Of lark and linnet, and from every page
　　Rise odours of ploughed field or flowery mead.

Edgar Allan Poe

1809–1849

Poe was the orphaned child of theatrical parents, raised by a rich
Virginia merchant. He grew up in England and Richmond, attended
the University of Virginia briefly, and, disastrously, West Point.
He was publishing characteristic verse by the age of twenty, and
supported himself as an editor and journalist from an early age. His
stories and literary criticism are more accomplished than his poems.
However, it is useful to attempt to see the poems through the sym-
bolist spectacles of Baudelaire, who admired and translated them;
past the jingling rhythm one is able to glimpse the dark wood of the
hidden self, which was to become the locale of much modernist
poetry.

A Dream within a Dream

Take this kiss upon the brow!
And, in parting from you now,
Thus much let me avow:
You are not wrong, who deem
That my days have been a dream;
Yet if Hope has flown away
In a night, or in a day,
In a vision, or in none,
Is it therefore the less *gone?*
All that we see or seem
Is but a dream within a dream.

I stand amid the roar
Of a surf-tormented shore,
And I hold within my hand
Grains of the golden sand—
How few! yet how they creep
Through my fingers to the deep,
While I weep—while I weep!
O God! can I not grasp
Them with a tighter clasp?
O God! can I not save

One from the pitiless wave?
Is *all* that we see or seem
But a dream within a dream?

Ulalume—A Ballad

The skies they were ashen and sober;
 The leaves they were crispéd and sere—
 The leaves they were withering and sere:
It was night, in the lonesome October
 Of my most immemorial year:
It was hard by the dim lake of Auber,
 In the misty mid region of Weir—
It was down by the dank tarn of Auber,
 In the ghoul-haunted woodland of Weir.

Here once, through an alley Titanic,
 Of cypress, I roamed with my Soul—
 Of cypress, with Psyche, my Soul.
These were days when my heart was volcanic
 As the scoriac rivers that roll—
 As the lavas that restlessly roll
Their sulphurous currents down Yaanek
 In the ultimate climes of the Pole—
That groan as they roll down Mount Yaanek
 In the realms of the Boreal Pole.

Our talk had been serious and sober,
 But our thoughts they were palsied and sere—
 Our memories were treacherous and sere;
For we knew not the month was October,
 And we marked not the night of the year
 (Ah, night of all nights in the year!)—
We noted not the dim lake of Auber
 (Though once we had journeyed down here)—
We remembered not the dank tarn of Auber,
 Nor the ghoul-haunted woodland of Weir.

And now, as the night was senescent
 And star-dials pointed to morn—

As the star-dials hinted of morn—
At the end of our path a liquescent
And nebulous lustre was born,
Out of which a miraculous crescent
Arose with a duplicate horn—
Astarte's bediamonded crescent
Distinct with its duplicate horn.

And I said: 'She is warmer than Dian;
She rolls through an ether of sighs—
She revels in a region of sighs.
She has seen that the tears are not dry on
These cheeks, where the worm never dies,
And has come past the stars of the Lion,
To point us the path to the skies—
To the Lethean peace of the skies—
Come up, in despite of the Lion,
To shine on us with her bright eyes—
Come up through the lair of the Lion,
With love in her luminous eyes.'

But Psyche, uplifting her finger,
Said: 'Sadly this star I mistrust—
Her pallor I strangely mistrust:
Ah, hasten!—ah, let us not linger:
Ah, fly!—let us fly!—for we must.'
In terror she spoke, letting sink her
Wings till they trailed in the dust—
In agony sobbed, letting sink her
Plumes till they trailed in the dust—
Till they sorrowfully trailed in the dust.

I replied: 'This is nothing but dreaming:
Let us on by this tremulous light!
Let us bathe in this crystalline light!
Its Sibyllic splendour is beaming
With Hope and in Beauty to-night:—
See!—it flickers up the sky through the night!
Ah, we safely may trust to its gleaming,
And be sure it will lead us aright—

[44]

We surely may trust to a gleaming,
    That cannot but guide us aright,
    Since it flickers up to Heaven through the night.'

Thus I pacified Psyche and kissed her,
    And tempted her out of her gloom—
    And conquered her scruples and gloom;
And we passed to the end of the vista,
    But were stopped by the door of a tomb—
    By the door of a legended tomb;
And I said: 'What is written, sweet sister,
    On the door of this legended tomb?'
    She replied: 'Ulalume—Ulalume!—
    'Tis the vault of thy lost Ulalume!'

Then my heart it grew ashen and sober
    As the leaves that were crispéd and sere—
    As the leaves that were withering and sere;
And I cried: 'It was surely October
    On *this* very night of last year
    That I journeyed—I journeyed down here!—
    That I brought a dread burden down here—
    On this night of all nights in the year,
    Ah, what demon hath tempted me here?
Well I know, now, this dim lake of Auber—
    This misty mid region of Weir—
Well I know, now, this dank tarn of Auber,
    This ghoul-haunted woodland of Weir.'

Said we, then—the two, then: 'Ah, can it
    Have been that the woodlandish ghouls—
    The pitiful, the merciful ghouls—
To bar up our way and to ban it
    From the secret that lies in these wolds—
    From the thing that lies hidden in these wolds—
Have drawn up the spectre of a planet
    From the limbo of lunary souls—
This sinfully scintillant planet
    From the Hell of the planetary souls?'

[45]

John Greenleaf Whittier

1807–1892

A Quaker and a bachelor, Whittier lived a tranquil life with the exception of the period in which he worked for the abolition of slavery. He wrote often of a rural life, and appealed to the nostalgia of a populace which was leaving the farm for the city.

Telling the Bees

Here is the place; right over the hill
　　Runs the path I took;
You can see the gap in the old wall still,
　　And the stepping-stones in the shallow brook.

There is the house, with the gate red-barred,
　　And the poplars tall;
And the barn's brown length, and the cattle-yard,
　　And the white horns tossing above the wall.

There are the beehives ranged in the sun;
　　And down by the brink
Of the brook are her poor flowers, weed-o'errun,
　　Pansy and daffodil, rose and pink.

A year has gone, as the tortoise goes,
　　Heavy and slow;
And the same rose blows, and the same sun glows,
　　And the same brook sings of a year ago.

There's the same sweet clover-smell in the breeze;
　　And the June sun warm
Tangles his wings of fire in the trees,
　　Setting, as then, over Fernside farm.

I mind me how with a lover's care
　　From my Sunday coat
I brushed off the burrs, and smoothed my hair,
　　And cooled at the brookside my brow and throat.

[46]

Since we parted, a month had passed,—
   To love, a year;
Down through the beeches I looked at last
   On the little red gate and the well-sweep near.

I can see it all now,—the slantwise rain
   Of light through the leaves,
The sundown's blaze on her window-pane,
   The bloom of her roses under the eaves.

Just the same as a month before,—
   The house and the trees,
The barn's brown gable, the vine by the door,—
   Nothing changed but the hives of bees.

Before them, under the garden wall,
   Forward and back,
Went drearily singing the chore-girl small,
   Draping each hive with a shred of black.

Trembling, I listened: the summer sun
   Had the chill of snow;
For I knew she was telling the bees of one
   Gone on the journey we all must go!

Then I said to myself, 'My Mary weeps
   For the dead to-day:
Haply her blind old grandsire sleeps
   The fret and the pain of his age away.'

But her dog whined low; on the doorway sill,
   With his cane to his chin,
The old man sat; and the chore-girl still
   Sung to the bees stealing out and in.

And the song she was singing ever since
   In my ear sounds on:—
'Stay at home, pretty bees, fly not hence!
   Mistress Mary is dead and gone!'

[47]

Jones Very
1813–1880

Very's poems were little read until Yvor Winters reprinted him in his critical book about American literature, *Maule's Curse*, in 1938. A friend of Emerson's, Very was a recluse and a mystic. He spent some time in an asylum for the insane.

The Latter Rain

The latter rain,—it falls in anxious haste
Upon the sun-dried fields and branches bare,
Loosening with searching drops the rigid waste,
As if it would each root's lost strength repair;
But not a blade grows green as in the spring,
No swelling twig puts forth its thickening leaves;
The robins only mid the harvests sing,
Pecking the grain that scatters from the sheaves:
The rain falls still,—the fruit all ripened drops,
It pierces chestnut burr and walnut shell,
The furrowed fields disclose the yellow crops,
Each bursting pod of talents used can tell,
And all that once received the early rain
Declare to man it was not sent in vain.

The Garden

I saw the spot where our first parents dwelt;
And yet it wore to me no face of change,
For while amid its fields and groves, I felt
As if I had not sinned, nor thought it strange;
My eye seemed but a part of every sight,
My ear heard music in each sound that rose;
Each sense forever found a new delight,
Such as the spirit's vision only knows;
Each act some new and ever-varying joy
Did by my Father's love for me prepare;

To dress the spot my ever fresh employ,
And in the glorious whole with Him to share;
No more without the flaming gate to stray,
No more for sin's dark stain the debt of death to pay.

Henry David Thoreau

1817–1862

Thoreau's writing in prose is considerably more distinguished than his verse. A friend of Emerson, he lived in his house and knew other transcendentalists, but himself was a separate and lonely figure. His *Walden* is deservedly his most celebrated book, and his lecture on 'Civil Disobedience' is an early monument of one of the best features of the American character.

Sic Vita

I am a parcel of vain strivings tied
    By a chance bond together,
Dangling this way and that, their links
    Were made so loose and wide,
        Methinks,
      For milder weather.

A bunch of violets without their roots,
    And sorrel intermixed,
    Encircled by a wisp of straw
      Once coiled about their shoots,
        The law
      By which I'm fixed.

A nosegay which Time clutched from out
    Those fair Elysian fields,
    With weeds and broken stems, in haste,
      Doth make the rabble rout
        That waste
      The day he yields.

And here I bloom for a short hour unseen,
    Drinking my juices up,
    With no root in the land
      To keep my branches green,
        But stand
      In a bare cup.

[50]

Some tender buds were left upon my stem
    In mimicry of life,
  But ah! the children will not know,
    Till time has withered them,
       The woe
     With which they're rife.

But now I see I was not plucked for naught,
    And after in life's vase
  Of glass set while I might survive,
    But by a kind hand brought
       Alive
     To a strange place.

That stock thus thinned will soon redeem its hours,
    And by another year,
  Such as God knows, with freer air,
    More fruits and fairer flowers
       Will bear,
     While I droop here.

Herman Melville

1819–1891

The author of *Moby Dick* wrote a number of good poems, but saved the best of himself for prose. When his greatest writing brought him little reward or praise, he virtually stopped writing, and was an anonymous customs inspector in New York from 1866–1885.

The Maldive Shark

About the Shark, phlegmatical one,
Pale sot of the Maldive sea,
The sleek little pilot-fish, azure and slim,
How alert in attendance be.
From his saw-pit of mouth, from his charnel of maw
They have nothing of harm to dread,
But liquidly glide on his ghastly flank
Or before his Gorgonian head;
Or lurk in the port of serrated teeth
In white triple tiers of glittering gates,
And there find a haven when peril's abroad,
An asylum in jaws of the Fates!
They are friends; and friendly they guide him to prey,
Yet never partake of the treat—
Eyes and brains to the dotard lethargic and dull,
Pale ravener of horrible meat.

Walt Whitman

1819–1892

Whitman, the son of a labourer, worked as a carpenter, school-teacher and journalist. After he began to write his poems, he performed as a male nurse around Washington during the Civil War, and held government sinecures. For most of his life as a poet, he managed to survive without regular employment. Despite the praise of Emerson and a few discriminating English readers, Whitman was generally unread in his own lifetime, though he enjoyed the adoration of a number of disciples. Frequently his poems were attacked obscene, because of his relative frankness about bodies. (see pp. 13–14)

I Saw in Louisiana a Live-Oak Growing

I saw in Louisiana a live-oak growing,
All alone stood it and the moss hung down from the branches,
Without any companion it grew there uttering joyous leaves of
    dark green,
And its look, rude, unbending, lusty, made me think of myself,
But I wonder'd how it could utter joyous leaves standing alone
    there without its friend near, for I knew I could not,
And I broke off a twig with a certain number of leaves upon it, and
    twined around it a little moss,
And brought it away, and I have placed it in sight in my room,
It is not needed to remind me as of my own dear friends,
(For I believe lately I think of little else than of them,)
Yet it remains to me a curious token, it makes me think of manly
    love;
For all that, and though the live-oak glistens there in Louisiana
    solitary in a wide flat space,
Uttering joyous leaves all its life without a friend a lover near,
I know very well I could not.

Out of the Cradle Endlessly Rocking

Out of the cradle endlessly rocking,
Out of the mocking-bird's throat, the musical shuttle,

Out of the Ninth-month midnight,
Over the sterile sands and the fields beyond, where the child leaving
    his bed wander'd alone, bareheaded, barefoot,
Down from the shower'd halo,
Up from the mystic play of shadows twining and twisting as if they
    were alive,
Out from the patches of briers and blackberries,
From the memories of the bird that chanted to me,
From your memories sad brother, from the fitful risings and fallings
    I heard,
From under that yellow half-moon late-risen and swollen as if with
    tears,
From those beginning notes of yearning and love there in the mist,
From the thousand responses of my heart never to cease,
From the myriad thence-arous'd words,
From the word stronger and more delicious than any,
From such as now they start the scene revisiting,
As a flock, twittering, rising, or overhead passing,
Borne hither, ere all eludes me, hurriedly,
A man, yet by these tears a little boy again,
Throwing myself on the sand, confronting the waves,
I, chanter of pains and joys, uniter of here and hereafter,
Taking all hints to use them, but swiftly leaping beyond them,
A reminiscence sing.

Once Paumanok,
When the lilac-scent was in the air and Fifth-month grass was
    growing,
Up this seashore in some briers,
Two feather'd guests from Alabama, two together,
And their nest, and four light-green eggs spotted with brown,
And every day the he-bird to and fro near at hand,
And every day the she-bird crouch'd on her nest, silent, with bright
    eyes,
And every day I, a curious boy, never too close, never disturbing
    them,
Cautiously peering, absorbing, translating.

Shine! shine! shine!
Pour down your warmth, great sun!

[54]

While we bask, we two together.

Two together!
Winds blow south, or winds blow north,
Day come white, or night come black,
Home, or rivers and mountains from home,
Singing all time, minding no time,
While we two keep together.

Till of a sudden,
May-be kill'd, unknown to her mate,
One forenoon the she-bird crouch'd not on the nest,
Nor return'd that afternoon, nor the next,
Nor ever appear'd again.

And thenceforward all summer in the sound of the sea,
And at night under the full of the moon in calmer weather,
Over the hoarse surging of the sea,
Or flitting from brier to brier by day,
I saw, I heard at intervals the remaining one, the he-bird,
The solitary guest from Alabama.

Blow! blow! blow!
Blow up sea-winds along Paumanok's shore;
I wait and I wait till you blow my mate to me.

Yes, when the stars glisten'd,
All night long on the prong of a moss-scallop'd stake,
Down almost amid the slapping waves,
Sat the lone singer wonderful causing tears.

He call'd on his mate,
He pour'd forth the meanings which I of all men know.

Yes my brother I know,
The rest might not, but I have treasur'd every note,
For more than once dimly down to the beach gliding,
Silent, avoiding the moonbeams, blending myself with the shadows,
Recalling now the obscure shapes, the echoes, the sounds and sights
    after their sorts,

The white arms out in the breakers tirelessly tossing,
I, with bare feet, a child, the wind wafting my hair,
Listen'd long and long.

Listen'd to keep, to sing, now translating the notes,
Following you my brother.

Soothe! soothe! soothe!
Close on its wave soothes the wave behind,
And again another behind embracing and lapping, every one close,
But my love soothes not me, not me.

Low hangs the moon, it rose late,
It is lagging—O I think it is heavy with love, with love.

O madly the sea pushes upon the land,
With love, with love.

O night! do I not see my love fluttering out among the breakers?
What is that little black thing I see there in the white?

Loud! loud! loud!
Loud I call to you, my love!

High and clear I shoot my voice over the waves,
Surely you must know who is here, is here,
You must know who I am, my love.

Low-hanging moon!
What is that dusky spot in your brown yellow?
O it is the shape, the shape of my mate!
O moon do not keep her from me any longer.

Land! land! O land!
Whichever way I turn, O I think you could give me my mate back again
*   if you only would,*
For I am almost sure I see her dimly whichever way I look.

O rising stars!
Perhaps the one I want so much will rise, will rise with some of you.

[56]

O throat! O trembling throat!
Sound clearer through the atmosphere!
Pierce the woods, the earth,
Somewhere listening to catch you must be the one I want.

Shake out carols!
Solitary here, the night's carols!
Carols of lonesome love! death's carols!
Carols under that lagging, yellow, waning moon!
O under that moon where she droops almost down into the sea!
O reckless despairing carols.

But soft! sink low!
Soft! let me just murmur,
And do you wait a moment you husky-nois'd sea,
For somewhere I believe I heard my mate responding to me,
So faint, I must be still, be still to listen,
But not altogether still, for then she might not come immediately to me.

Hither my love!
Here I am! here!
With this just-sustain'd note I announce myself to you,
This gentle call is for you my love, for you.

Do not be decoy'd elsewhere,
That is the whistle of the wind, it is not my voice,
That is the fluttering, the fluttering of the spray,
Those are the shadows of leaves.

O darkness! O in vain!
O I am very sick and sorrowful.

O brown halo in the sky near the moon, drooping upon the sea!
O troubled reflection in the sea!
O throat! O throbbing heart!
And I singing uselessly, uselessly all the night.

O past! O happy life! O songs of joy!
In the air, in the woods, over fields,
Loved! loved! loved! loved! loved!

But my mate no more, no more with me!
We two together no more.

The aria sinking,
All else continuing, the stars shining,
The winds blowing, the notes of the bird continuous echoing,
With angry moans the fierce old mother incessantly moaning,
On the sands of Paumanok's shore gray and rustling,
The yellow half-moon enlarged, sagging down, drooping, the face
    of the sea almost touching,
The boy ecstatic, with his bare feet the waves, with his hair the
    atmosphere dallying,
The love in the heart long pent, now loose, now at last tumultuously
    bursting,
The aria's meaning, the ears, the soul, swiftly depositing,
The strange tears down the cheeks coursing,
The colloquy there, the trio, each uttering,
The undertone, the savage old mother incessantly crying,
To the boy's soul's questions sullenly timing, some drown'd secret
    hissing,
To the outsetting bard.

Demon or bird! (said the boy's soul,)
Is it indeed toward your mate you sing? or is it really to me?
For I, that was a child, my tongue's use sleeping, now I have heard
    you,
Now in a moment I know what I am for, I awake,
And already a thousand singers, a thousand songs, clearer, louder
    and more sorrowful than yours,
A thousand warbling echoes have started to life within me, never
    to die.

O you singer solitary, singing by yourself, projecting me,
O solitary me listening, never more shall I cease perpetuating you,
Never more shall I escape, never more the reverberations,
Never more the cries of unsatisfied love be absent from me,
Never again leave me to be the peaceful child I was before what
    there in the night,
By the sea under the yellow and sagging moon,
The messenger there arous'd, the fire, the sweet hell within,
The unknown want, the destiny of me.

O give me the clew! (it lurks in the night here somewhere,)
O if I am to have so much, let me have more!

A word then, (for I will conquer it,)
The word final, superior to all,
Subtle, sent up—what is it?—I listen;
Are you whispering it, and have been all the time, you sea-waves?
Is that it from your liquid rims and wet sands?

Whereto answering, the sea,
Delaying not, hurrying not,
Whisper'd me through the night, and very plainly before daybreak,
Lisp'd to me the low and delicious word death,
And again death, death, death, death,
Hissing melodious, neither like the bird nor like my arous'd child's
    heart,
But edging near as privately for me rustling at my feet,
Creeping thence steadily up to my ears and laving me softly all over,
Death, death, death, death, death.

Which I do not forget,
But fuse the song of my dusky demon and brother,
That he sang to me in the moonlight on Paumanok's gray beach,
With the thousand responsive songs at random,
My own songs awaked from that hour,
And with them the key, the word up from the waves,
The word of the sweetest song and all songs,
That strong and delicious word which, creeping to my feet,
(Or like some old crone rocking the cradle, swathed in sweet
    garments, bending aside,)
The sea whisper'd me.

The Dalliance of the Eagles

Skirting the river road, (my forenoon walk, my rest,)
Skyward in air a sudden muffled sound, the dalliance of the eagles,
The rushing amorous contact high in space together,
The clinching interlocking claws, a living, fierce, gyrating wheel,
Four beating wings, two beaks, a swirling mass tight grappling,

In tumbling turning clustering loops, straight downward falling,
Till o'er the river pois'd, the twain yet one, a moment's lull,
A motionless still balance in the air, then parting, talons loosing,
Upward again on slow-firm pinions slanting, their separate diverse
    flight,
She hers, he his, pursuing.

A Farm Picture

    Through the ample open door of the peaceful country barn,
    A sunlit pasture field with cattle and horses feeding,
    And haze and vista, and the far horizon fading away.

An Army Corps on the March

With its cloud of skirmishers in advance,
With now the sound of a single shot snapping like a whip, and now
    an irregular volley,
The swarming ranks press on and on, the dense brigades press on,
Glittering dimly, toiling under the sun—the dust-cover'd men,
In columns rise and fall to the undulations of the ground,
With artillery interspers'd—the wheels rumble, the horses sweat,
As the army corps advances.

By the Bivouac's Fitful Flame

By the bivouac's fitful flame,
A procession winding around me, solemn and sweet and slow—but
    first I note,
The tents of the sleeping army, the fields' and woods' dim outline,
The darkness lit by spots of kindled fire, the silence,
Like a phantom far or near an occasional figure moving,
The shrubs and trees, (as I lift my eyes they seem to be stealthily
    watching me,)
While wind in procession thoughts, O tender and wondrous
    thoughts,

Of life and death, of home and the past and loved, and of those that
    are far away;
A solemn and slow procession there as I sit on the ground,
By the bivouac's fitful flame.

When Lilacs Last in the Dooryard Bloom'd

1

When lilacs last in the dooryard bloom'd,
And the great star early droop'd in the western sky in the night,
I mourn'd, and yet shall mourn with ever-returning spring.

Ever-returning spring, trinity sure to me you bring,
Lilac blooming perennial and drooping star in the west,
And thought of him I love.

2

O powerful western fallen star!
O shades of night—O moody, tearful night!
O great star disappear'd—O the black murk that hides the star!
O cruel hands that hold me powerless—O helpless soul of me!
O harsh surrounding cloud that will not free my soul.

3

In the dooryard fronting an old farm-house near the white-wash'd
    palings,
Stands the lilac-bush tall-growing with heart-shaped leaves of rich
    green,
With many a pointed blossom rising delicate, with the perfume
    strong I love,
With every leaf a miracle—and from this bush in the dooryard,
With delicate-color'd blossoms and heart-shaped leaves of rich
    green,
A sprig with its flower I break.

4

In the swamp in secluded recesses,
A shy and hidden bird is warbling a song.

Solitary the thrush,
The hermit withdrawn to himself, avoiding the settlements,
Sings by himself a song.

Song of the bleeding throat,
Death's outlet song of life, (for well dear brother I know,
If thou wast not granted to sing thou would'st surely die.)

5

Over the breast of the spring, the land, amid cities,
Amid lanes and through old woods, where lately the violets peep'd
    from the ground, spotting the gray debris,
Amid the grass in the fields each side of the lanes, passing the endless
    grass,
Passing the yellow-spear'd wheat, every grain from its shroud in
    the dark-brown fields uprisen,
Passing the apple-tree blows of white and pink in the orchards,
Carrying a corpse to where it shall rest in the grave,
Night and day journeys a coffin.

6

Coffin that passes through lanes and streets,
Through day and night with the great cloud darkening the land,
With the pomp of the inloop'd flags with the cities draped in black,
With the show of the States themselves as of crape-veil'd women
    standing,
With processions long and winding and the flambeaus of the night,
With the countless torches lit, with the silent sea of faces and the
    unbared heads,
With the waiting depot, the arriving coffin, and the sombre faces,
With dirges through the night, with the thousand voices rising
    strong and solemn,
With all the mournful voices of the dirges pour'd around the coffin,
The dim-lit churches and the shuddering organs—where amid these
    you journey,
With the tolling tolling bells' perpetual clang,
Here, coffin that slowly passes,
I give you my sprig of lilac.

7

(Nor for you, for one alone,
Blossoms and branches green to coffins all I bring,
For fresh as the morning, thus would I chant a song for you O sane
    and sacred death.

All over bouquets of roses,
O death, I cover you over with roses and early lilies,
But mostly and now the lilac that blooms the first,
Copious I break, I break the sprigs from the bushes,
With loaded arms I come, pouring for you,
For you and the coffins all of you O death.)

8

O western orb sailing the heaven,
Now I know what you must have meant as a month since I walk'd,
As I walk'd in silence the transparent shadowy night,
As I saw you had something to tell as you bent to me night after
    night,
As you droop'd from the sky low down as if to my side, (while the
    other stars all look'd on,)
As we wander'd together the solemn night, (for something I know
    not what kept me from sleep,)
As the night advanced, and I saw on the rim of the west how full
    you were of woe,
As I stood on the rising ground in the breeze in the cool transparent
    night,
As I watch'd where you pass'd and was lost in the netherward black
    of the night,
As my soul in its trouble dissatisfied sank, as where you sad orb,
Concluded, dropt in the night, and was gone.

9

Sing on there in the swamp,
O singer bashful and tender, I hear your notes, I hear your call,
I hear, I come presently, I understand you,
But a moment I linger, for the lustrous star has detain'd me,
The star my departing comrade holds and detains me.

10

O how shall I warble myself for the dead one there I loved?
And how shall I deck my song for the large sweet soul that has gone?
And what shall my perfume be for the grave of him I love?

Sea-winds blown from east and west,
Blown from the Eastern sea and blown from the Western sea, till
there on the prairies meeting,
These and with these and the breath of my chant,
I'll perfume the grave of him I love.

11

O what shall I hang on the chamber walls?
And what shall the pictures be that I hang on the walls,
To adorn the burial-house of him I love?

Pictures of growing spring and farms and homes,
With the Fourth-month eve at sundown, and the gray smoke lucid
and bright,
With floods of the yellow gold of the gorgeous, indolent, sinking
sun, burning, expanding the air,
With the fresh sweet herbage under foot, and the pale green leaves
of the trees prolific,
In the distance the flowing glaze, the breast of the river, with a
wind-dapple here and there,
With ranging hills on the banks, with many a line against the sky,
and shadows,
And the city at hand with dwellings so dense, and stacks of chimneys,
And all the scenes of life and the workshops, and the workmen
homeward returning.

12

Lo, body and soul—this land,
My own Manhattan with spires, and the sparkling and hurrying
tides, and the ships,
The varied and ample land, the South and the North in the light,
Ohio's shores and flashing Missouri,
And ever the far-spreading prairies cover'd with grass and corn.

Lo, the most excellent sun so calm and haughty,
The violet and purple morn with just-felt breezes,
The gentle soft-born measureless light,
The miracle spreading bathing all, the fulfill'd noon,
The coming eve delicious, the welcome night and the stars,
Over my cities shining all, enveloping man and land.

13

Sing on, sing on you gray-brown bird,
Sing from the swamps, the recesses, pour your chant from the
    bushes,
Limitless out of the dusk, out of the cedars and pines.

Sing on dearest brother, warble your reedy song,
Loud human song, with voice of uttermost woe.

O liquid and free and tender!
O wild and loose to my soul—O wondrous singer!
You only I hear—yet the star holds me, (but will soon depart,)
Yet the lilac with mastering odor holds me.

14

Now while I sat in the day and look'd forth,
In the close of the day with its light and the fields of spring, and the
    farmers preparing their crops,
In the large unconscious scenery of my land with its lakes and
    forests,
In the heavenly aerial beauty, (after the perturb'd winds and the
    storms,)
Under the arching heavens of the afternoon swift passing, and the
    voices of children and women,
The many-moving sea-tides, and I saw the ships how they sail'd,
And the summer approaching with richness, and the fields all busy
    with labour,
And the infinite separate houses, how they all went on, each with
    its meals and minutia of daily usages,
And the streets how their throbbings throbb'd, and the cities pent
    —lo, then and there,
Falling upon them all and among them all, enveloping me with the
    rest,

Appear'd the cloud, appear'd the long black trail,
And I knew death, its thought, and the sacred knowledge of death.

Then with the knowledge of death as walking one side of me,
And the thought of death close-walking the other side of me,
And I in the middle as with companions, and as holding the hands
    of companions,
I fled forth to the hiding receiving night that talks not,
Down to the shores of the water, the path by the swamp in the
    dimness,
To the solemn shadowy cedars and ghostly pines so still.

And the singer so shy to the rest receiv'd me,
The gray-brown bird I know receiv'd us comrades three,
And he sang the carol of death, and a verse for him I love.

From deep secluded recesses,
From the fragrant cedars and the ghostly pines so still,
Came the carol of the bird.

And the charm of the carol rapt me,
As I held as if by their hands my comrades in the night,
And the voice of my spirit tallied the song of the bird.

Come lovely and soothing death,
Undulate round the world, serenely arriving, arriving,
In the day, in the night, to all, to each,
Sooner or later delicate death.

Prais'd be the fathomless universe,
For life and joy, and for objects and knowledge curious,
And for love, sweet love—but praise! praise! praise!
For the sure-enwinding arms of cool-enfolding death.

Dark mother always gliding near with soft feet,
Have none chanted for thee a chant of fullest welcome?
Then I chant it for thee, I glorify thee above all,
I bring thee a song that when thou must indeed come, come unfalteringly.

Approach strong deliveress,
When it is so, when thou hast taken them I joyously sing the dead,

[66]

Lost in the loving floating ocean of thee,
Laved in the flood of thy bliss O death.

From me to thee glad serenades,
Dances for thee I propose saluting thee, adornments and feastings for thee,
And the sights of the open landscape and the high-spread sky are fitting,
And life and the fields, and the huge and thoughtful night.

The night in silence under many a star,
The ocean shore and the husky whispering wave whose voice I know,
And the soul turning to thee O vast and well-veil'd death,
And the body gratefully nestling close to thee.

Over the tree-tops I float thee a song,
Over the rising and sinking waves, over the myriad fields and the prairies
*   wide,*
Over the dense-pack'd cities all and the teeming wharves and ways,
I float this carol with joy, with joy to thee O death.

15

To the tally of my soul,
Loud and strong kept up the gray-brown bird,
With pure deliberate notes spreading filling the night.

Loud in the pines and cedars dim,
Clear in the freshness moist and the swamp-perfume,
And I with my comrades there in the night.

While my sight that was bound in my eyes unclosed,
As to long panoramas of visions.

And I saw askant the armies,
I saw as in noiseless dreams hundreds of battle-flags,
Borne through the smoke of the battles and pierc'd with missiles
      I saw them,
And carried hither and yon through the smoke, and torn and bloody,
And at last but a few shreds left on the staffs, (and all in silence,)
And the staffs all splinter'd and broken.

I saw battle-corpses, myriads of them,
And the white skeletons of young men, I saw them,
I saw the debris and debris of all the slain soldiers of the war,
But I saw they were not as was thought,
They themselves were fully at rest, they suffer'd not,
The living remain'd and suffer'd, the mother suffer'd,
And the wife and the child and the musing comrade suffer'd,
And the armies that remain'd suffer'd.

16

Passing the visions, passing the night,
Passing, unloosing the hold of my comrades' hands,
Passing the song of the hermit bird and the tallying song of my soul,
Victorious song, death's outlet song, yet varying ever-altering song,
As low and wailing, yet clear the notes, rising and falling, flooding
    the night,
Sadly sinking and fainting, as warning and warning, and yet again
    bursting with joy,
Covering the earth and filling the spread of the heaven,
As that powerful psalm in the night I heard from recesses,
Passing, I leave thee lilac with heart-shaped leaves,
I leave thee there in the door-yard, blooming, returning with spring.

I cease from my song for thee,
From my gaze on thee in the west, fronting the west, communing
    with thee,
O comrade lustrous with silver face in the night.

Yet each to keep and all, retrievements out of the night,
The song, the wondrous chant of the gray-brown bird,
And the tallying chant, the echo arous'd in my soul,
With the lustrous and drooping star with the countenance full of
    woe,
With the holders holding my hand nearing the call of the bird,
Comrades mine and I in the midst, and their memory ever to keep,
    for the dead I loved so well,
For the sweetest, wisest soul of all my days and lands—and this for
    his dear sake,
Lilac and star and bird twined with the chant of my soul,
There in the fragrant pines and the cedars dusk and dim.

Frederick Goddard Tuckerman

1821–1873

Another recluse, Tuckerman lived most of his life in solitude in Greenfield, Massachusetts. His poems were collected in 1931, after sixty-odd years of neglect.

1:5

And so the day drops by; the horizon draws
The fading sun, and we stand struck in grief;
Failing to find our haven of relief,—
Wide of the way, nor sure to turn or pause;
And weep to view how fast the splendour wanes,
And scarcely heed, that yet some share remains
Of the red after-light, some time to mark,
Some space between the sundown and the dark.
But not for him those golden calms succeed,
Who, while the day is high and glory reigns,
Sees it go by,—as the dim Pampas plain,
Hoary with salt, and gray with bitter weed,
Sees the vault blacken, feels the dark wind strain,
Hears the dry thunder roll, and knows no rain.

1:17

All men,—the preacher saith,—whate'er or whence
Their increase, walking through this world has been;
Both those that gather out, or after-glean,
Or hold in simple fee of harvests dense;
Or but perhaps a flowerless barren green,
Barren with spots of sorrel, knot-grass, spurge:—
See to one end their differing paths converge,
And all must render answer, here or hence.
'Lo, Death is at the doors,' he crieth, 'with blows!'
But what to him unto whose feverish sense
The stars tick audibly, and the wind's low surge
In the pine, attended, tolls, and throngs, and grows
On the dread ear,—a thunder too profound
For bearing,—a Niagara of sound!

Emily Dickinson
1830–1886

After the age of thirty-two, Emily Dickinson seldom left her room in her father's house in Amherst, Massachusetts. She dressed in white and wrote her complex, extraordinary poems with little sense that anyone would ever read them (which accounts for their fragmentary notation). She had been educated at Mount Holyoke, and had fallen in love as some of her poems indicate, but no one knows the details of her intensely private life. Early in her career as a poet, she attempted to publish and was largely rebuffed. When her poems were first printed after her death, the editors polished and altered them. It was not until 1958 that an accurate and complete edition became available. (See pp. 14–16.)

341*

After great pain, a formal feeling comes—
The Nerves sit ceremonious, like Tombs—
The stiff Heart questions was it He, that bore,
And Yesterday, or Centuries before?

The Feet, mechanical, go round—
Of Ground, or Air, or Ought—
A Wooden way
Regardless grown,
A Quartz contentment, like a stone—

This is the Hour of Lead—
Remembered, if outlived,
As Freezing persons, recollect the Snow—
First—Chill—then Stupor—then the letting go—

465

I heard a Fly buzz—when I died—
The Stillness in the Room

* The poems are numbered in the 1958 text.

Was like the Stillness in the Air—
Between the Heaves of Storm—

The Eyes around—had wrung them dry—
And Breaths were gathering firm
For that last Onset—when the King
Be witnessed—in the Room—

I willed my Keepsakes—Signed away
What portion of me be
Assignable—and then it was
There interposed a Fly—

With Blue—uncertain stumbling Buzz—
Between the light—and me—
And then the Windows failed—and then
I could not see to see—

512

The Soul has Bandaged moments—
When too appalled to stir—
She feels some ghastly Fright come up
And stop to look at her—

Salute her—with long fingers—
Caress her freezing hair—
Sip, Goblin, from the very lips
The Lover—hovered—o'er—
Unworthy, that a thought so mean
Accost a Theme—so—fair—

The soul has moments of Escape—
When bursting all the doors—
She dances like a Bomb, abroad,
And swings upon the Hours,

As do the Bee—delirious borne—
Long Dungeoned from his Rose—

Touch Liberty—then know no more,
But Noon, and Paradise—

The Soul's retaken moments—
When, Felon led along,
With shackles on the plumed feet,
And staples, in the Song,

The Horror welcomes her, again,
These, are not brayed of Tongue—

536

The Heart asks Pleasure—first—
And then—Excuse from Pain—
And then—those little Anodynes
That deaden suffering—

And then—to go to sleep—
And then—if it should be
The will of its Inquisitor
The privilege to die—

640

I cannot live with You—
It would be Life—
And Life is over there—
Behind the Shelf

The Sexton keeps the Key to—
Putting up
Our Life—His Porcelain—
Like a Cup—

Discarded of the Housewife—
Quaint—or Broke—
A newer Sevres pleases—
Old Ones crack—

I could not die—with You—
For One must wait
To shut the Other's Gaze down—
You—could not—

And I—Could I stand by
And see You—freeze—
Without my Right of Frost—
Death's privilege?

Nor could I rise—with You—
Because Your Face
Would put out Jesus'—
That New Grace

Glow plain—and foreign
On my homesick Eye—
Except that You than He
Shone closer by—

They'd judge Us—How—
For You—served Heaven—You know,
Or sought to—
I could not—

Because You saturated Sight—
And I had no more Eyes
For sordid excellence
As Paradise

And were You lost, I would be—
Though My Name
Rang loudest
On the Heavenly fame—

And were You—saved—
And I—condemned to be
Where You were not—
That self—were Hell to Me—

So We must meet apart—
You there—I—here—
With just the Door ajar
That Oceans are—and Prayer—
And that White Sustenance—
Despair—

1068

Further in Summer than the Birds
Pathetic from the Grass
A minor Nation celebrates
It's unobtrusive Mass.

No Ordinance be seen
So gradual the Grace
A pensive Custom it becomes
Enlarging Loneliness.

Antiquest felt at Noon
When August burning low
Arise this spectral Canticle
Repose to typify

Remit as yet no Grace
No Furrow on the Glow
Yet a Druidic Difference
Enhances Nature now

1333

A little Madness in the Spring
Is wholesome even for the King,
But God be with the Clown—
Who ponders this tremendous scene—
This whole Experiment of Green—
As if it were his own!

1397

It sounded as if the Streets were running
And then—the Streets stood still—
Eclipse—was all we could see at the Window
And Awe—was all we could feel.

By and by—the boldest stole out of his Covert
To see if Time was there—
Nature was in an Opal Apron,
Mixing fresher Air.

1445

Death is the supple Suitor
That wins at last—
It is a stealthy Wooing
Conducted first
By pallid innuendoes
And dim approach
But brave at last with Bugles
And a bisected Coach
It bears away in triumph
To Troth unknown
And Kinsmen as divulgeless
As throngs of Down—

1732

My life closed twice before its close;
It yet remains to see
If Immortality unveil
A third event to me,

So huge, so hopeless to conceive
As these that twice befel.
Parting is all we know of heaven,
And all we need of hell.

Sidney Lanier

1842–1881

A native of Georgia, Lanier served in the Confederate Army and contracted tuberculosis in a Union prison. He supported himself by performing as a flautist, and wrote an important work of theoretical prosody (*The Science of English Verse*) as well as fiction and poetry.

The Raven Days

Our hearths are gone out, and our hearts are broken,
    And but the ghosts of homes to us remain,
And ghostly eyes and hollow sighs give token
    From friend to friend of an unspoken pain.

O, Raven Days, dark Raven Days of sorrow,
    Bring to us, in your whetted ivory beaks,
Some sign out of the far land of To-morrow,
    Some strip of sea-green dawn, some orange streaks.

Ye float in dusky files, forever croaking—
    Ye chill our manhood with your dreary shade.
Pale, in the dark, not even God invoking,
    We lie in chains, too weak to be afraid.

O Raven Days, dark Raven Days of sorrow,
    Will ever any warm light come again?
Will ever the lit mountains of To-morrow
    Begin to gleam across the mournful plain?

Struggle

My Soul is like the oar that momently
    Dies in a desperate stress beneath the wave,
Then glitters out again and sweeps the sea:
    Each second I'm new-born from some new grave.

[76]

Duncan Campbell Scott
1862–1947

Duncan Campbell Scott was the first Canadian poet of distinction.
He was born in Ottawa, educated in Canada, and worked for the
Canadian government. He wrote short stories as well as poems.

The Sailor's Sweetheart

O if love were had for asking
  In the markets of the town,
Hardly a lass would think to wear
  A fine silken gown:
But love is had by grieving
By choosing and by leaving,
And there's no one now to ask me
If heavy lies my heart.

O if love were had for a deep wish
  In the deadness of the night,
There'd be a truce to longing
  Between the dusk and the light:
But love is had for sighing,
For living and for dying,
And there's no one now to ask me
If heavy lies my heart.

O if love were had for taking
  Like honey from the hive,
The bees that made the tender stuff
  Could hardly keep alive:
But love it is a wounded thing,
A tremor and a smart,
And there's no one left to kiss me now
Over my heavy heart.

A Song

In the air there are no coral—
  Reefs or ambergris,
No rock-pools that hide the lovely
  Sea-anemones,
No strange forms that flow with phosphor
  In a deep-sea night,
No slow fish that float their colour
  Through the liquid light,
No young pearls, like new moons, growing
  Perfect in their shells;
If you be in search of beauty
  Go where beauty dwells.

In the sea there are no sunsets
  Crimson in the west,
No dark pines that hold the shadow
  On the mountain-crest,
There is neither mist nor moonrise
  Rainbows nor rain,
No sweet flowers that in the autumn
  Die to bloom again,
Music never moves the silence,—
  Reeds or silver bells;
If you be in search of beauty
  Go where beauty dwells.

Edgar Lee Masters

1868–1950

A practising lawyer in Chicago, Masters published a dozen volumes
of unremarkable verse before his *Spoon River Anthology* of 1915,
from which the following poems are taken. He never equalled the
success of this book, though he continued to write prolifically.

The Hill

Where are Elmer, Herman, Bert, Tom and Charley,
The weak of will, the strong of arm, the clown, the boozer, the
    fighter?
All, all, are sleeping on the hill.

One passed in a fever,
One was burned in a mine,
One was killed in a brawl,
One died in a jail,
One fell from a bridge toiling for children and wife—
All, all are sleeping, sleeping, sleeping on the hill.

Where are Ella, Kate, Mag, Lizzie and Edith,
The tender heart, the simple soul, the loud, the proud, the happy
    one?—
All, all, are sleeping on the hill.

One died in shameful child-birth,
One of a thwarted love,
One at the hands of a brute in a brothel,
One of a broken pride, in the search for heart's desire,
One after life in far-away London and Paris
Was brought to her little space by Ella and Kate and Mag—
All, all are sleeping, sleeping, sleeping on the hill.

Where are Uncle Isaac and Aunt Emily,
And old Towny Kincaid and Sevigne Houghton,
And Major Walker who had talked

With venerable men of the revolution?—
All, all, are sleeping on the hill.

They brought them dead sons from the war,
And daughters whom life had crushed,
And their children fatherless, crying—
All, all are sleeping, sleeping, sleeping on the hill.

Where is Old Fiddler Jones
Who played with life all his ninety years,
Braving the sleet with bared breast,
Drinking, rioting, thinking neither of wife nor kin,
Nor gold, nor love, nor heaven?
Lo! he babbles of the fish-frys of long ago,
Of the horse-races of long ago at Clary's Grove,
Of what Abe Lincoln said
One time at Springfield.

English Thornton

Here! You sons of the men
Who fought with Washington at Valley Forge,
And whipped Black Hawk at Starved Rock,
Arise! Do battle with the descendants of those
Who bought land in the loop when it was waste sand,
And sold blankets and guns to the army of Grant,
And sat in legislatures in the early days,
Taking bribes from the railroads!
Arise! Do battle with the fops and bluffs,
The pretenders and figurantes of the society column,
And the yokel souls whose daughters marry counts;
And the parasites on great ideas,
And the noisy riders of great causes,
And the heirs of ancient thefts.
Arise! And make the city yours,
And the State yours—
You who are sons of the hardy yeomanry of the forties!
By God! If you do not destroy these vermin
My avenging ghost will wipe out
Your city and your state.

Edwin Arlington Robinson
1869–1935

Robinson grew up in Gardiner, Maine, which became, locale and populace, the source of much of his poetry. His early work, though excellent (some of his best-known work was published while he was an undergraduate at Harvard), was too realistic for an audience that would only accept pretty verses. Robinson became an alcoholic and a derelict, and was rescued by a remarkable circumstance: President Theodore Roosevelt came into possession of a privately printed volume of Robinson, admired it, offered Robinson a government sinecure, and bullied his publishers into taking Robinson on. Success came quickly. Robinson spent summers at the MacDowell colony in Peterborough, New Hampshire, and winters in his bachelor apartment in New York. He took up drinking again, late in life, as a protest against prohibition.

Luke Havergal

Go to the western gate, Luke Havergal,
There where the vines cling crimson on the wall,
And in the twilight wait for what will come.
The leaves will whisper there of her, and some,
Like flying words, will strike you as they fall;
But go, and if you listen she will call.
Go to the western gate, Luke Havergal—
Luke Havergal.

No, there is not a dawn in eastern skies
To rift the fiery night that's in your eyes;
But there, where western glooms are gathering,
The dark will end the dark, if anything:
God slays Himself with every leaf that flies,
And hell is more than half of paradise.
No, there is not a dawn in eastern skies—
In eastern skies.

Out of a grave I come to tell you this,
Out of a grave I come to quench the kiss
That flames upon your forehead with a glow
That blinds you to the way that you must go.
Yes, there is yet one way to where she is,
Bitter, but one that faith may never miss.
Out of a grave I come to tell you this—
To tell you this.

There is the western gate, Luke Havergal,
There are the crimson leaves upon the wall.
Go, for the winds are tearing them away,—
Nor think to riddle the dead words they say,
Nor any more to feel them as they fall;
But go, and if you trust her she will call.
There is the western gate, Luke Havergal—
Luke Havergal.

The Poor Relation

No longer torn by what she knows
And sees within the eyes of others,
Her doubts are when the daylight goes,
Her fears are for the few she bothers.
She tells them it is wholly wrong
Of her to stay alive so long;
And when she smiles her forehead shows
A crinkle that had been her mother's.

Beneath her beauty, blanched with pain,
And wistful yet for being cheated,
A child would seem to ask again
A question many times repeated;
But no rebellion has betrayed
Her wonder at what she has paid
For memories that have no stain,
For triumph born to be defeated.

To those who come for what she was—
The few left who know where to find her—

She clings, for they are all she has;
And she may smile when they remind her,
As theretofore, of what they know
Of roses that are still to blow
By ways where not so much as grass
Remains of what she sees behind her.

They stay a while, and having done
What penance or the past requires,
They go, and leave her there alone
To count her chimneys and her spires.
Her lip shakes when they go away,
And yet she would not have them stay;
She knows as well as anyone
That Pity, having played, soon tires.

But one friend always reappears,
A good ghost, not to be forsaken;
Whereat she laughs and has no fears
Of what a ghost may reawaken,
But welcomes, while she wears and mends
The poor relation's odds and ends,
Her truant from a tomb of years—
Her power of youth so early taken.

Poor laugh, more slender than her song
It seems; and there are none to hear it
With even the stopped ears of the strong
For breaking heart or broken spirit.
The friends who clamoured for her place,
And would have scratched her for her face,
Have lost her laughter for so long
That none would care enough to fear it.

None live who need fear anything
From her, whose losses are their pleasure;
The plover with a wounded wing
Stays not the flight that others measure;
So there she waits, and while she lives,
And death forgets, and faith forgives,

Her memories go foraging
For bits of childhood song they treasure.

And like a giant harp that hums
On always, and is always blending
The coming of what never comes
With what has past and had an ending,
The City trembles, throbs, and pounds
Outside, and through a thousand sounds
The small intolerable drums
Of Time are like slow drops descending.

Bereft enough to shame a sage
And given little to long sighing,
With no illusion to assuage
The lonely changelessness of dying,—
Unsought, unthought-of, and unheard,
She sings and watches like a bird,
Safe in a comfortable cage
From which there will be no more flying.

Eros Turannos*

She fears him, and will always ask
    What fated her to choose him;
She meets in his engaging mask
    All reason to refuse him;
But what she meets and what she fears
Are less than are the downward years,
Drawn slowly to the foamless weirs
    Of age, were she to lose him.

Between a blurred sagacity
    That once had power to sound him,
And Love, that will not let him be
    The Judas that she found him,

* Love the Tyrant.

[84]

Her pride assuages her almost,
As if it were alone the cost.—
He sees that he will not be lost,
    And waits and looks around him.

A sense of ocean and old trees
    Envelops and allures him;
Tradition, touching all he sees,
    Beguiles and reassures him;
And all her doubts of what he says
Are dimmed with what she knows of days—
Till even prejudice delays
    And fades, and she secures him.

The falling leaf inaugurates
    The reign of her confusion:
The pounding wave reverberates
    The dirge of her illusion;
And home, where passion lived and died,
Becomes a place where she can hide,
While all the town and harbour side
    Vibrate with her seclusion.

We tell you, tapping on our brows,
    The story as it should be,—
As if the story of a house
    Were told, or ever could be;
We'll have no kindly veil between
Her visions and those we have seen,—
As if we guessed what hers have been,
    Or what they are or would be.

Meanwhile we do no harm; for they
    That with a god have striven,
Not hearing much of what we say,
    Take what the god has given;
Though like waves breaking it may be,
Or like a changed familiar tree,
Or like a stairway to the sea
    Where down the blind are driven.

[85]

Hillcrest

(*To Mrs. Edward MacDowell*)

No sound of any storm that shakes
Old island walls with older seas
Comes here where now September makes
An island in a sea of trees.

Between the sunlight and the shade
A man may learn till he forgets
The roaring of a world remade,
And all his ruins and regrets;

And if he still remembers here
Poor fights he may have won or lost,—
If he be ridden with the fear
Of what some other fight may cost,—

If, eager to confuse too soon,
What he has known with what may be,
He reads a planet out of tune
For cause of his jarred harmony,—

If here he venture to unroll
His index of adagios,
And he be given to console
Humanity with what he knows,—

He may by contemplation learn
A little more than what he knew,
And even see great oaks return
To acorns out of which they grew.

He may, if he but listen well,
Through twilight and the silence here,
Be told what there are none may tell
To vanity's impatient ear;

[86]

And he may never dare again
Say what awaits him, or be sure
What sunlit labyrinth of pain
He may not enter and endure.

Who knows to-day from yesterday
May learn to count no thing too strange:
Love builds of what Time takes away,
Till Death itself is less than Change.

Who sees enough in his duress
May go as far as dreams have gone;
Who sees a little may do less
Than many who are blind have done;

Who sees unchastened here the soul
Triumphant has no other sight
Than has a child who sees the whole
World radiant with his own delight.

Far journeys and hard wandering
Awaits him in whose crude surmise
Peace, like a mask, hides everything
That is and has been from his eyes;

And all his wisdom is unfound,
Or like a web that error weaves
On airy looms that have a sound
No louder now than falling leaves.

Trumbull Stickney
1874–1904

Born the same year as Robert Frost, dead of a brain tumour almost sixty years before Frost's death, Stickney is one of the great unfulfilled talents of America. He was also a scholar, the first American to take a doctorate in literature at the Sorbonne. He was teaching at Harvard when he died, part of the Harvard generation of the 90s, which included William Vaughn Moody, that promised much and accomplished little.

Mnemosyne

It's autumn in the country I remember.

How warm a wind blew here about the ways!
And shadows on the hillside lay to slumber
During the long sun-sweetened summer-days.

It's cold abroad the country I remember.

The swallows veering skimmed the golden grain
At midday with a wing aslant and limber;
And yellow cattle browsed upon the plain.

It's empty down the country I remember.

I had a sister lovely in my sight:
Her hair was dark, her eyes were very sombre;
We sang together in the woods at night.

It's lonely in the country I remember.

The babble of our children fills my ears,
And on our hearth I stare the perished ember
To flames that show all starry thro' my tears.

It's dark about the country I remember.

There are the mountains where I lived. The path
Is slushed with cattle-tracks and fallen timber,
The stumps are twisted by the tempests' wrath.

But that I knew these places are my own,
I'd ask how came such wretchedness to cumber
The earth, and I to people it alone.

It rains across the country I remember.

Mt. Lykaion

Alone on Lykaion since man hath been
Stand on the height two columns, where at rest
Two eagles hewn of gold sit looking East
Forever; and the sun goes up between.
Far down around the mountain's oval green
An order keeps the falling stones abreast.
Below within the chaos last and least
A river like a curl of light is seen.
Beyond the river lies the even sea,
Beyond the sea another ghost of sky,—
O God, support the sickness of my eye
Lest the far space and long antiquity
Suck out my heart, and on this awful ground
The great wind kill my little shell with sound.

Dramatic Fragment

Sir, say no more.
Within me 't is as if
The green and climbing eyesight of a cat
Crawled near my mind's poor birds.

Robert Frost

1874–1963

The most popular figure in American poetry, Robert Frost was born in San Francisco but lived in New England for all but ten of his eighty-eight years. For a more complete account, see the Introduction to this book (pp. 16–19).

The Pasture

I'm going out to clean the pasture spring;
I'll only stop to rake the leaves away
(And wait to watch the water clear, I may):
I sha'n't be gone long.—You come too.

I'm going out to fetch the little calf
That's standing by the mother. It's so young
It totters when she licks it with her tongue.
I sha'n't be gone long.—You come too.

After Apple-Picking

My long two-pointed ladder's sticking through a tree
Toward heaven still,
And there's a barrel that I didn't fill
Beside it, and there may be two or three
Apples I didn't pick upon some bough.
But I am done with apple-picking now.
Essence of winter sleep is on the night,
The scent of apples: I am drowsing off.
I cannot rub the strangeness from my sight
I got from looking through a pane of glass
I skimmed this morning from the drinking trough
And held against the world of hoary grass.
It melted, and I let it fall and break.
But I was well
Upon my way to sleep before it fell,

And I could tell
What form my dreaming was about to take.
Magnified apples appear and disappear
Stem end and blossom end,
And every fleck of russet showing clear.
My instep arch not only keeps the ache,
It keeps the pressure of a ladder-round.
I feel the ladder sway as the boughs bend.
And I keep hearing from the cellar bin
The rumbling sound
Of load on load of apples coming in.
For I have had too much
Of apple-picking: I am overtired
Of the great harvest I myself desired.
There were ten thousand thousand fruit to touch,
Cherish in hand, lift down, and not let fall.
For all
That struck the earth,
No matter if not bruised or spiked with stubble,
Went surely to the cider-apple heap
As of no worth.
One can see what will trouble
This sleep of mine, whatever sleep it is.
Were he not gone,
The woodchuck could say whether it's like his
Long sleep, as I describe its coming on,
Or just some human sleep.

'Out, out—'

The buzz-saw snarled and rattled in the yard
And made dust and dropped stove-length sticks of wood,
Sweet-scented stuff when the breeze drew across it.
And from there those that lifted eyes could count
Five mountain ranges one behind the other
Under the sunset far into Vermont.
And the saw snarled and rattled, snarled and rattled,
As it ran light, or had to bear a load.
And nothing happened: day was all but done.

Call it a day, I wish they might have said
To please the boy by giving him the half hour
That a boy counts so much when saved from work.
His sister stood beside them in her apron
To tell them 'Supper.' At the word, the saw,
As if to prove saws knew what supper meant,
Leaped out at the boy's hand, or seemed to leap—
He must have given the hand. However it was,
Neither refused the meeting. But the hand!
The boy's first outcry was a rueful laugh,
As he swung toward them holding up the hand
Half in appeal, but half as if to keep
The life from spilling. Then the boy saw all—
Since he was old enough to know, big boy
Doing a man's work, though a child at heart—
He saw all spoiled. 'Don't let him cut my hand off—
The doctor, when he comes. Don't let him, sister!'
So. But the hand was gone already.
The doctor put him in the dark of ether.
He lay and puffed his lips out with his breath.
And then—the watcher at his pulse took fright.
No one believed. They listened at his heart.
Little—less—nothing!—and that ended it.
No more to build on there. And they, since they
Were not the one dead, turned to their affairs.

Stopping by Woods on a Snowy Evening

Whose woods these are I think I know.
His house is in the village though;
He will not see me stopping here
To watch his woods fill up with snow.

My little horse must think it queer
To stop without a farmhouse near
Between the woods and frozen lake
The darkest evening of the year.

He gives his harness bells a shake
To ask if there is some mistake.

The only other sound's the sweep
Of easy wind and downy flake.

The woods are lovely, dark and deep,
But I have promises to keep,
And miles to go before I sleep,
And miles to go before I sleep.

To Earthward

Love at the lips was touch
As sweet as I could bear;
And once that seemed too much;
I lived on air

That crossed me from sweet things,
The flow of—was it musk
From hidden grapevine springs
Down hill at dusk?

I had the swirl and ache
From sprays of honeysuckle
That when they're gathered shake
Dew on the knuckle.

I craved strong sweets, but those
Seemed strong when I was young;
The petal of the rose
It was that stung.

Now no joy but lacks salt
That is not dashed with pain
And weariness and fault;
I crave the stain

Of tears, the aftermark
Of almost too much love,
The sweet of bitter bark
And burning clove.

[93]

When stiff and sore and scarred
I take away my hand
From leaning on it hard
In grass and sand,

The hurt is not enough:
I long for weight and strength
To feel the earth as rough
To all my length.

Design

I found a dimpled spider, fat and white,
On a white heal-all, holding up a moth
Like a white piece of rigid satin cloth—
Assorted characters of death and blight
Mixed ready to begin the morning right,
Like the ingredients of a witches' broth—
A snow-drop spider, a flower like froth,
And dead wings carried like a paper kite.

What had that flower to do with being white,
The wayside blue and innocent heal-all?
What brought the kindred spider to that height,
Then steered the white moth thither in the night?
What but design of darkness to appall?—
If design govern in a thing so small.

Desert Places

Snow falling and night falling fast, oh, fast
In a field I looked into going past,
And the ground almost covered smooth in snow,
But a few weeds and stubble showing last.

The woods around it have it—it is theirs.
All animals are smothered in their lairs.
I am too absent-spirited to count;
The loneliness includes me unawares.

And lonely as it is that loneliness
Will be more lonely ere it will be less—
A blanker whiteness of benighted snow
With no expression, nothing to express.

They cannot scare me with their empty spaces
Between stars—on stars where no human race is.
I have it in me so much nearer home
To scare myself with my own desert places.

The Most of It

He thought he kept the universe alone;
For all the voice in answer he could wake
Was but the mocking echo of his own
From some tree-hidden cliff across the lake.
Some morning from the boulder-broken beach
He would cry out on life, that what it wants
Is not its own love back in copy speech,
But counter-love, original response.
And nothing ever came of what he cried
Unless it was the embodiment that crashed
In the cliff's talus on the other side,
And then in the far distant water splashed.
But after a time allowed for it to swim,
Instead of proving human when it neared
And someone else additional to him,
As a great buck it powerfully appeared,
Pushing the crumpled water up ahead,
And landed pouring like a waterfall,
And stumbled through the rocks with horny tread,
And forced the underbrush—and that was all.

The Draft Horse

With a lantern that wouldn't burn
In too frail a buggy we drove
Behind too heavy a horse
Through a pitch-dark limitless grove.

And a man came out of the trees
And took our horse by the head
And reaching back to his ribs
Deliberately stabbed him dead.

The ponderous beast went down
With a crack of a broken shaft.
And the night drew through the trees
In one long invidious draft.

The most unquestioning pair
That ever accepted fate
And the least disposed to ascribe
Any more than we had to to hate,

We assumed that the man himself
Or someone he had to obey
Wanted us to get down
And walk the rest of the way.

Vachel Lindsay
1879–1931

Lindsay, a midwestern poet, is best-known for long chants which he delivered to audiences fervently and with considerable success. When his popularity diminished he became despondent, and ended his life by drinking poison.

The Flower-Fed Buffaloes

The flower-fed buffaloes of the spring
In the days of long ago,
Ranged where the locomotives sing
And the prairie flowers lie low:
The tossing, blooming, perfumed grass
Is swept away by wheat,
Wheels and wheels and wheels spin by
In the spring that still is sweet.
But the flower-fed buffaloes of the spring
Left us long ago.
They gore no more, they bellow no more,
They trundle around the hills no more:—
With the Blackfeet lying low,
With the Pawnees lying low.

Factory Windows Are Always Broken

Factory windows are always broken.
Somebody's always throwing bricks,
Somebody's always heaving cinders,
Playing ugly Yahoo tricks.

Factory windows are always broken.
Other windows are let alone.
No one throws through the chapel-window
The bitter, snarling derisive stone.

Factory windows are always broken.
Something or other is going wrong.
Something is rotten—I think, in Denmark.
End of the factory-window song.

Wallace Stevens

1879–1955

Stevens spent most of his life as Vice-President of Hartford Accident and Indemnity Insurance Company, writing delicate symbolist poems in his spare time. He trained as a lawyer, and in his youth lived in New York where he knew William Carlos Williams, Alfred Kreymbourg and other American poets who had not joined the expatriate exodus. Most of his life was resolutely anti-poetic (he is alleged to have said, on one of the rare occasions when he read his poems in public, 'If the boys in the office could see me now—!') while the material of his poetry was the most rarified speculation about the nature of imagination and reality. (See pp. 19-22.)

The Emperor of Ice-Cream

Call the roller of big cigars,
The muscular one, and bid him whip
In kitchen cups concupiscent curds.
Let the wenches dawdle in such dress
As they are used to wear, and let the boys
Bring flowers in last month's newspapers.
Let it be finale of seem.
The only emperor is the emperor of ice-cream.

Take from the dresser of deal,
Lacking the three glass knobs, that sheet
On which she embroidered fantails once
And spread it so as to cover her face.
If her horny feet protrude, they come
To show how cold she is, and dumb.
Let the lamp affix its beam.
The only emperor is the emperor of ice-cream.

Disillusionment of Ten O'Clock

The houses are haunted
By white night-gowns.

None are green,
Or purple with green rings,
Or green with yellow rings,
Or yellow with blue rings.
None of them are strange,
With socks of lace
And beaded ceintures.
People are not going
To dream of baboons and periwinkles.
Only, here and there, an old sailor,
Drunk and asleep in his boots,
Catches tigers
In red weather.

Anecdote of the Jar

I placed a jar in Tennessee,
And round it was, upon a hill.
It made the slovenly wilderness
Surround that hill.

The wilderness rose up to it,
And sprawled around, no longer wild.
The jar was round upon the ground
And tall and of a port in air.

It took dominion everywhere.
The jar was gray and bare.
It did not give of bird or bush,
Like nothing else in Tennessee.

Sunday Morning

I

Complacencies of the peignoir, and late
Coffee and oranges in a sunny chair,
And the green freedom of a cockatoo
Upon a rug mingle to dissipate

The holy hush of ancient sacrifice.
She dreams a little, and she feels the dark
Encroachment of that old catastrophe,
As a calm darkens among water-lights.
The pungent oranges and bright, green wings
Seem things in some procession of the dead,
Winding across wide water, without sound.
The day is like wide water, without sound,
Stilled for the passing of her dreaming feet
Over the seas, to silent Palestine,
Dominion of the blood and sepulchre.

II

Why should she give her bounty to the dead?
What is divinity if it can come
Only in silent shadows and in dreams?
Shall she not find in comforts of the sun,
In pungent fruit and bright, green wings, or else
In any balm or beauty of the earth,
Things to be cherished like the thought of heaven?
Divinity must live within herself:
Passions of rain, or moods in falling snow;
Grievings in loneliness, or unsubdued
Elations when the forest blooms; gusty
Emotions on wet roads on autumn nights;
All pleasures and all pains, remembering
The bough of summer and the winter branch.
These are the measures destined for her soul.

III

Jove in the clouds had his inhuman birth.
No mother suckled him, no sweet land gave
Large-mannered motions to his mythy mind.
He moved among us, as a muttering king,
Magnificent, would move among his hinds,
Until our blood, commingling, virginal,
With heaven, brought such requital to desire
The very hinds discerned it, in a star.
Shall our blood fail? Or shall it come to be

The blood of paradise? And shall the earth
Seem all of paradise that we shall know?
The sky will be much friendlier then than now,
A part of labour and a part of pain,
And next in glory to enduring love,
Not this dividing and indifferent blue.

IV

She says, 'I am content when wakened birds,
Before they fly, test the reality
Of misty fields, by their sweet questionings;
But when the birds are gone, and their warm fields
Return no more, where, then, is paradise?'
There is not any haunt of prophecy,
Nor any old chimera of the grave,
Neither the golden underground, nor isle
Melodious, where spirits gat them home,
Nor visionary south, nor cloudy palm
Remote on heaven's hill, that has endured
As April's green endures; or will endure
Like her remembrance of awakened birds,
Or her desire for June and evening, tipped
By the consummation of the swallow's wings.

V

She says, 'But in contentment I still feel
The need of some imperishable bliss.'
Death is the mother of beauty; hence from her,
Alone, shall come fulfilment to our dreams
And our desires. Although she strews the leaves
Of sure obliteration on our paths,
The path sick sorrow took, the many paths
Where triumph rang its brassy phrase, or love
Whispered a little out of tenderness,
She makes the willow shiver in the sun
For maidens who were wont to sit and gaze
Upon the grass, relinquished to their feet.
She causes boys to pile new plums and pears
On disregarded plate. The maidens taste
And stay impassioned in the littering leaves.

VI

Is there no change of death in paradise?
Does ripe fruit never fall? Or do the boughs
Hang always heavy in that perfect sky,
Unchanging, yet so like our perishing earth,
With rivers like our own that seek for seas
They never find, the same receding shores
That never touch with inarticulate pang?
Why set the pear upon those river-banks
Or spice the shores with odors of the plum?
Alas, that they should wear our colors there,
The silken weavings of our afternoons,
And pick the strings of our insipid lutes!
Death is the mother of beauty, mystical,
Within whose burning bosom we devise
Our earthly mothers waiting, sleeplessly.

VII

Supple and turbulent, a ring of men
Shall chant in orgy on a summer morn
Their boisterous devotion to the sun,
Not as a god, but as a god might be,
Naked among them, like a savage source.
Their chant shall be a chant of paradise,
Out of their blood, returning to the sky;
And in their chant shall enter, voice by voice,
The windy lake wherein their lord delights,
The trees, like serafin, and echoing hills,
That choir among themselves long afterward.
They shall know well the heavenly fellowship
Of men that perish and of summer morn.
And whence they came and whither they shall go
The dew upon their feet shall manifest.

VIII

She hears, upon that water without sound,
A voice that cries, 'The tomb in Palestine
Is not the porch of spirits lingering.
It is the grave of Jesus, where he lay.'

We live in an old chaos of the sun,
Or old dependency of day and night,
Or island solitude, unsponsored, free,
Of that wide water, inescapable.
Deer walk upon our mountains, and the quail
Whistle about us their spontaneous cries;
Sweet berries ripen in the wilderness;
And, in the isolation of the sky,
At evening, casual flocks of pigeons make
Ambiguous undulations as they sink,
Downward to darkness, on extended wings.

The Idea of Order at Key West

She sang beyond the genius of the sea.
The water never formed to mind or voice,
Like a body wholly body, fluttering
Its empty sleeves; and yet its mimic motion
Made constant cry, caused constantly a cry,
That was not ours although we understood,
Inhuman, of the veritable ocean.

The sea was not a mask. No more was she.
The song and water were not medleyed sound
Even if what she sang was what she heard,
Since what she sang was uttered word by word.
It may be that in all her phrases stirred
The grinding water and the gasping wind;
But it was she and not the sea we heard.

For she was the maker of the song she sang.
The ever-hooded, tragic-gestured sea
Was merely a place by which she walked to sing.
Whose spirit is this? we said, because we knew
It was the spirit that we sought and knew
That we should ask this often as she sang.

If it was only the dark voice of the sea
That rose, or even colored by many waves;
If it was only the outer voice of sky

And cloud, of the sunken coral water-walled,
However clear, it would have been deep air,
The heaving speech of air, a summer sound
Repeated in a summer without end
And sound alone. But it was more than that,
More even than her voice, and ours, among
The meaningless plungings of water and the wind,
Theatrical distances, bronze shadows heaped
On high horizons, mountainous atmospheres
Of sky and sea.
             It was her voice that made
The sky acutest at its vanishing.
She measured to the hour its solitude.
She was the single artificer of the world
In which she sang. And when she sang, the sea,
Whatever self it had, became the self
That was her song, for she was the maker. Then we,
As we beheld her striding there alone,
Knew that there never was a world for her
Except the one she sang and, singing, made.

Ramon Fernandez, tell me, if you know,
Why, when the singing ended and we turned
Toward the town, tell why the glassy lights,
The lights in the fishing boats at anchor there,
As the night descended, tilting in the air,
Mastered the night and portioned out the sea,
Fixing emblazoned zones and fiery poles,
Arranging, deepening, enchanting night.

Oh! Blessed rage for order, pale Ramon,
The maker's rage to order words of the sea,
Words of the fragrant portals, dimly-starred,
And of ourselves and of our origins,
In ghostlier demarcations, keener sounds.

The Course of a Particular

Today the leaves cry, hanging on branches swept by wind,
Yet the nothingness of winter becomes a little less.
It is still full of icy shades and shapen snow.

The leaves cry . . . One holds off and merely hears the cry.
It is a busy cry, concerning someone else.
And though one says that one is part of everything,

There is a conflict, there is a resistance involved;
And being part is an exertion that declines:
One feels the life of that which gives life as it is.

The leaves cry. It is not a cry of divine attention,
Nor the smoke-drift of puffed-out heroes, nor human cry.
It is the cry of leaves that do not transcend themselves,

In the absence of fantasia, without meaning more
Than they are in the final finding of the air, in the thing
Itself, until, at last, the cry concerns no one at all.

William Carlos Williams
1883–1962

A practising physician in New Jersey, specializing in obstetrics, Williams nevertheless wrote novels, essays, stories, an autobiography, and an unusual quantity of good poems. He observes and commemorates the urban American life that he sees. His long poem *Paterson* (especially the first two books) includes many of the best passages of his work. He was devoted to the American idiom. Though a friend and admirer of Ezra Pound, he wished to establish localism as an alternative to Pound's internationalism; Eliot and *The Waste Land* were for Williams a catastrophe in the history of American poetry.

Portrait of a Lady

Your thighs are appletrees
whose blossoms touch the sky.
Which sky? The sky
where Watteau hung a lady's
slipper. Your knees
are a southern breeze—or
a gust of snow. Agh! what
sort of man was Fragonard?
—as if that answered
anything. Ah, yes—below
the knees, since the tune
drops that way, it is
one of those white summer days,
the tall grass of your ankles
flickers upon the shore—
Which shore?—
the sand clings to my lips—
Which shore?
Agh, petals maybe. How
should I know?
Which shore? Which shore?
I said petals from an appletree.

The Widow's Lament in Springtime

Sorrow is my own yard
where the new grass
flames as it has flamed
often before but not
with the cold fire
that closes round me this year.
Thirty-five years
I lived with my husband.
The plumtree is white today
with masses of flowers.
Masses of flowers
loaded the cherry branches
and colour some bushes
yellow and some red
but the grief in my heart
is stronger than they
for though they were my joy
formerly, today I notice them
and turned away forgetting.
Today my son told me
that in the meadows,
at the edge of the heavy woods
in the distance, he saw
trees of white flowers.
I feel that I would like
to go there
and fall into those flowers
and sink into the marsh near them.

Spring and All

By the road to the contagious hospital
under the surge of the blue
mottled clouds driven from the
northeast—a cold wind. Beyond, the

waste of broad, muddy fields
brown with dried weeds, standing and fallen

patches of standing water
the scattering of tall trees

All along the road the reddish
purplish, forked, upstanding, twiggy
stuff of bushes and small trees
with dead, brown leaves under them
leafless vines—

Lifeless in appearance, sluggish
dazed spring approaches—

They enter the new world naked,
cold, uncertain of all
save that they enter. All about them
the cold, familiar wind—

Now the grass, tomorrow
the stiff curl of wildcarrot leaf

One by one objects are defined—
It quickens: clarity, outline of leaf

But now the stark dignity of
entrance—Still, the profound change
has come upon them: rooted they
grip down and begin to awaken

The Yachts

contend in a sea which the land partly encloses
shielding them from the too heavy blows
of an ungoverned ocean which when it chooses

tortures the biggest hulls, the best man knows
to pit against it beatings, and sinks them pitilessly.
Mothlike in mists, scintillant in the minute

brilliance of cloudless days, with broad bellying sails
they glide to the wind tossing green water
from their sharp prows while over them the crew crawls

ant like, solicitously grooming them, releasing,
making fast as they turn, lean far over and having
caught the wind again, side by side, head for the mark.

In a well guarded arena of open water surrounded by
lesser and greater craft which, sycophant, lumbering
and flittering follow them, they appear youthful, rare

as the light of a happy eye, live with the grace
of all that in the mind is feckless, free and
naturally to be desired. Now the sea which holds them

is moody, lapping their glossy sides, as if feeling
for some slightest flaw but fails completely.
Today no race. Then the wind comes again. The yachts

move, jockeying for a start, the signal is set and they
are off. Now the waves strike at them but they are too
well made, they slip through, though they take in canvas.

Arms with hands grasping seek to clutch at the prows.
Bodies thrown recklessly in the way are cut aside.
It is a sea of faces about them in agony, in despair

until the horror of the race dawns staggering the mind,
the whole sea become an entanglement of watery bodies
lost to the world bearing what they cannot hold. Broken,

beaten, desolate, reaching from the dead to be taken up
they cry out, failing, failing! their cries rising
in waves still as the skillful yachts pass over.

Paterson: Episode 17

>   Beat hell out of it
>   Beautiful Thing
>   spotless cap

[110]

and crossed white straps
over the dark rippled cloth—
    Lift the stick
above that easy head
where you sit by the ivied
church, one arm
    buttressing you
long fingers spread out
among the clear grass prongs—
    and drive it down
    Beautiful Thing
that your caressing body kiss
    and kiss again
that holy lawn—

And again! obliquely—
legs curled under you as a
    deer's leaping—
pose of supreme indifference
    sacrament
to a summer's day
    Beautiful Thing
in the unearned suburbs
    then pause
    the arm fallen—
what memories
of what forgotten face
brooding upon that lily stem?

    The incredible
nose straight from the brow
    the empurpled lips
and dazzled half sleepy eyes
    Beautiful Thing
of some trusting animal
    makes a temple
of its place of savage slaughter
    revealing
the damaged will incites still
    to violence

consummately beautiful Thing
and falls about your resting
    shoulders—

Gently! Gently!
as in all things an opposite
    that awakes
the fury, conceiving
    knowledge
by way of despair that has
    no place
to lay its glossy head—
Save only—Not alone!
    Never, if possible
alone! to escape the accepted
    chopping block
and a square hat!—

And as reverie gains and
    your joints loosen
    the trick's done!
Day is covered and we see you—
    but not alone!
drunk and bedraggled to release
the strictness of beauty
under a sky full of stars
    Beautiful Thing
and a slow moon—

        The car
    had stopped long since
    when the others
came and dragged those out
    who had you there
    indifferent
to whatever the anesthetic
    Beautiful Thing
might slum away the bars—

Reek of it!
    What does it matter?
    could set free
only the one thing—
But you!
—in your white lace dress
    'the dying swan'
and high heeled slippers—tall
as you already were—
    till your head
through fruitful exaggeration
was reaching the sky and the
prickles of its ecstasy
    Beautiful Thing!

And the guys from Paterson
    beat up
the guys from Newark and told
them to stay the hell out
of their territory and then
socked you one
    across the nose
    Beautiful Thing
for good luck and emphasis
    cracking it
till I must believe that all
desired women have had each
    in the end
    a busted nose
and live afterward marked up
    Beautiful Thing
    for memory's sake
to be credible in their deeds

Then back to the party!
    and they maled
and femaled you jealously
    Beautiful Thing
as if to discover when and
    by what miracle

there should escape what?
still to be possessed
out of what part
    Beautiful Thing
should it look?
    or be extinguished—
Three days in the same dress
    up and down—

    It would take
A Dominie to be patient
    Beautiful Thing
with you—

The stroke begins again—
    regularly
automatic
    contrapuntal to
the flogging
like the beat of famous lines
in the few excellent poems
    woven to make you
    gracious
and on frequent occasions
    foul drunk
    Beautiful Thing
pulse of release
    to the attentive
and obedient mind.

E. J. Pratt
1883–1964

Pratt was born in Newfoundland and lived most of his life in Toronto, where he taught English at the University. On three occasions he won the Governor-General's Award for poetry.

The Prize Cat

Pure blood domestic, guaranteed,
Soft-mannered, musical in purr,
The ribbon had declared the breed,
Gentility was in the fur.

Such feline culture in the gads,
No anger ever arched her back—
What distance since those velvet pads
Departed from the leopard's track!

And when I mused how Time had thinned
The jungle strains within the cells,
How human hands had disciplined
Those prowling optic parallels;

I saw the generations pass
Along the reflex of a spring,
A bird had rustled in the grass,
The tab had caught it on the wing:

Behind the leap so furtive-wild
Was such ignition in the gleam,
I thought an Abyssinian child
Had cried out in the whitethroat's scream.

Come not the Seasons Here

Comes not the springtime here,
  Though the snowdrop came,
And the time of the cowslip is near,
  For a yellow flame
Was found in a tuft of green;
  And the joyous shout
  Of a child rang out
That a cuckoo's eggs were seen.

Comes not the summer here,
    Though the cowslip be gone,
Though the wild rose blow as the year
  Draws faithfully on;
Though the face of the poppy be red
  In the morning light,
  And the ground be white
With the bloom of the locust shed.

Comes not the autumn here,
  Though someone said
He found a leaf in the sere
  By an aster dead;
And knew that the summer was done,
  For a herdsman cried
That his pastures were brown in the sun,
  And his wells were dried.

Nor shall the winter come,
  Though the elm be bare,
And every voice be dumb
  On the frozen air;
But the flap of a waterfowl
  In the marsh alone,
Or the hoot of a horned owl
  On a glacial stone.

Ezra Pound

1885–

Pound grew up in Pennsylvania where he did graduate work at the University. Most of his adult life he has spent in England, France and especially Italy. For a more complete account, see the Introduction, pp. 22–24.

In a Station of the Metro

> The apparition of these faces in the crowd;
> Petals on a wet, black bough.

The River Merchant's Wife: A Letter

While my hair was still cut straight across my forehead
I played about the front gate, pulling flowers.
You came by on bamboo stilts, playing horse,
You walked about my seat, playing with blue plums.
And we went on living in the village of Chokan:
Two small people, without dislike or suspicion.

At fourteen I married My Lord you.
I never laughed, being bashful.
Lowering my head, I looked at the wall.
Called to, a thousand times, I never looked back.

At fifteen I stopped scowling,
I desired my dust to be mingled with yours
Forever and forever and forever.
Why should I climb the look out?

At sixteen you departed,
You went into far Ku-to-yen, by the river of swirling
      eddies,
And you have been gone five months.
The monkeys make sorrowful noise overhead.

[117]

You dragged your feet when you went out.
By the gate now, the moss is grown, the different mosses,
Too deep to clear them away!
The leaves fall early this autumn, in wind.
The paired butterflies are already yellow with August
Over the grass in the West garden;
They hurt me. I grow older.
If you are coming down through the narrows of the river
    Kiang,
Please let me know beforehand,
And I will come out to meet you
        As far as Cho-fu-Sa.

From *Hugh Selwyn Mauberley*

I

E.P. ode pour l'élection de son sépulchre

For three years, out of key with his time,
He strove to resuscitate the dead art
Of poetry; to maintain 'the sublime'
In the old sense. Wrong from the start—

No hardly, but, seeing he had been born
In a half savage country, out of date;
Bent resolutely on wringing lilies from the acorn;
Capaneus; trout for factitious bait;

Ἴδμεν γάρ τοι πάνθ', ὅσ' ἐνὶ Τροίῃ
Caught in the unstopped ear;
Giving the rocks small lee-way
The chopped seas held him, therefore, that year.

His true Penelope was Flaubert,
He fished by obstinate isles;
Observed the elegance of Circe's hair
Rather than the mottoes on sun-dials.

Unaffected by 'the march of events,'
He passed from men's memory in *l'an trentiesme*
De son eage; the case presents
No adjunct to the Muses' diadem.

II

The age demanded an image
Of its accelerated grimace,
Something for the modern stage,
Not, at any rate, an Attic grace;

Not, not certainly, the obscure reveries
Of the inward gaze;
Better mendacities
Than the classics in paraphrase!

The 'age demanded' chiefly a mould in plaster,
Made with no loss of time,
A prose kinema, not, not assuredly, alabaster
Or the 'sculpture' of rhyme.

III

The tea-rose tea-gown, etc.
Supplants the mousseline of Cos,
The pianola 'replaces'
Sappho's barbitos.

Christ follows Dionysus,
Phallic and ambrosial
Made way for macerations;
Caliban casts out Ariel.

All things are a flowing,
Sage Heracleitus says;
But a tawdry cheapness
Shall outlast our days.

Even the Christian beauty
Defects—after Samothrace;
We see τὸ καλὸν
Decreed in the market place.

[119]

Faun's flesh is not to us,
Nor the saint's vision.
We have the press for wafer;
Franchise for circumcision.

All men, in law, are equals,
Free of Pisistratus,
We choose a knave or an eunuch
To rule over us.

O bright Apollo,
τίν' ἄνδρα, τίν, ἥρωα, τίνα θεον,
What god, man, or hero,
Shall I place a tin wreath upon!

IV

These fought in any case,
   and some believing,
            pro domo, in any case . . .

Some quick to arm,
some for adventure,
some from fear of weakness,
some from fear of censure,
some for love of slaughter, in imagination,
learning later . . .
some in fear, learning love of slaughter;

Died some, pro patria,
           non 'dulce' non 'et decor' . . .
walked eye-deep in hell
believing in old men's lies, then unbelieving
came home, home to a lie,
home to many deceits,
home to old lies and new infamy;
usury age-old and age-thick
and liars in public places.

Daring as never before, wastage as never before.
Young blood and high blood,
fair cheeks, and fine bodies;

fortitude as never before

frankness as never before,
disillusions as never told in the old days,
hysterias, trench confessions,
laughter out of dead bellies.

v

There died a myriad,
And of the best, among them,
For an old bitch gone in the teeth,
For a botched civilization,

Charm, smiling at the good mouth,
Quick eyes gone under earth's lid,

For two gross of broken statues,
For a few thousand battered books.

Canto 1

And then went down to the ship,
Set keel to breakers, forth on the godly sea, and
We set up mast and sail on that swart ship,
Bore sheep aboard her, and our bodies also
Heavy with weeping, so winds from sternward
Bore us out onward with bellying canvas,
Circe's this craft, the trim-coifed goddess.
Then sat we amidships, wind jamming the tiller,
Thus with stretched sail, we went over sea till day's end.
Sun to his slumber, shadows o'er all the ocean,
Came we then to the bounds of deepest water,
To the Kimmerian lands, and peopled cities
Covered with close-webbed mist, unpiercéd ever
With glitter of sun-rays
Nor with stars stretched, nor looking back from heaven
Swartest night stretched over wretched men there.

The ocean flowing backward, came we then to the place
Aforesaid by Circe.
Here did they rites, Perimedes and Eurylochus,
And drawing sword from my hip
I dug the ell-square pitkin;
Poured we libations unto each the dead,
First mead and then sweet wine, water mixed with white flour.
Then prayed I many a prayer to the sickly death's-heads;
As set in Ithaca, sterile bulls of the best
For sacrifice, heaping the pyre with goods,
A sheep to Tiresias only, black and a bell-sheep.
Dark blood flowed in the fosse,
Souls out of Erebus, cadaverous dead, of brides,
Of youths and of the old who had borne much;
Souls stained with recent tears, girls tender,
Men many, mauled with bronze lance heads,
Battle spoil, bearing yet dreory arms,
These many crowded about me; with shouting,
Pallor upon me, cried to my men for more beasts;
Slaughtered the herds, sheep slain of bronze;
Poured ointment, cried to the gods,
To Pluto the strong, and praised Proserpine;
Unsheathed the narrow sword,
I sat to keep off the impetuous impotent dead,
Till I should hear Tiresias.
But first Elpenor came, our friend Elpenor,
Unburied, cast on the wide earth,
Limbs that we left in the house of Circe,
Unwept, unwrapped in sepulchre, since toils urged other.
Pitiful spirit. And I cried in hurried speech:
'Elpenor, how art thou come to this dark coast?
'Cam'st thou afoot, outstripping seamen?'
          And he in heavy speech:
'Ill fate and abundant wine. I slept in Circe's ingle.
'Going down the long ladder unguarded,

'I fell against the buttress,
'Shattered the nape-nerve, the soul sought Avernus.
'But thou, O King, I bid remember me, unwept, unburied,
'Heap up mine arms, be tomb by sea-bord, and inscribed:

'A man of no fortune, and with a name to come.
'And set my oar up, that I swung mid fellows.'

And Anticlea came, whom I beat off, and then Tiresias Theban,
Holding his golden wand, knew me, and spoke first:
'A second time? why? man of ill star,
'Facing the sunless dead and this joyless region?
'Stand from the fosse, leave me my bloody bever
'For soothsay.'
   And I stepped back,
And he strong with the blood, said then: 'Odysseus
'Shalt return through spiteful Neptune, over dark seas,
'Lose all companions.' Then Anticlea came.
Lie quiet Divus. I mean, that is Andreas Divus,
In officina Wecheli, 1538, out of Homer.
And he sailed, by Sirens and thence outward and away
And unto Circe.
   Venerandam,
In the Cretan's phrase, with the golden crown, Aphrodite,
Cypri munimenta sortita est, mirthful, oricalchi, with
  golden
 Girdles and breast bands, thou with dark eyelids
 Bearing the golden bough of Argicida. So that:

H. D.

1886–1961

Hilda Doolittle was a friend of Ezra Pound and William Carlos
Williams at the University of Pennsylvania. She went to Europe in
1911, where she lived thenceforth, and became an Imagist. She
married the English poet Richard Aldington.

Heat

O wind, rend open the heat,
cut apart the heat,
rend it to tatters.

Fruit cannot drop
through this thick air—
fruit cannot fall into heat
that presses up and blunts
the points of pears
and rounds the grapes.

Cut the heat—
plough through it,
turning it on either side
of your path.

Orchard

I saw the first pear
as it fell—
the honey-seeking, golden-banded,
the yellow swarm
was not more fleet than I,
(spare us from loveliness)
and I fell prostrate
crying:
you have flayed us

with your blossoms,
spare us the beauty
of fruit-trees.

The honey-seeking
paused not,
the air thundered their song,
and I alone was prostrate.

O rough-hewn
god of the orchard,
I bring you an offering—
do you, alone unbeautiful,
son of the god,
spare us from loveliness:

these fallen hazel-nuts,
stripped late of their green sheaths,
grapes, red-purple,
their berries
dripping with wine,
pomegranates already broken,
and shrunken figs
and quinces untouched,
I bring you as offering.

Robinson Jeffers
1887–1962

After a broad education, Jeffers progressively withdrew from modern America, and from humanity itself. He built himself a stone house and tower in Carmel, California, and lived out his life facing the Pacific.

To the Stone-Cutters

Stone-cutters fighting time with marble, you fore-defeated
Challengers of oblivion
Eat cynical earnings, knowing rock splits, records fall down,
The square-limbed Roman letters
Scale in the thaws, wear in the rain. The poet as well
Builds his monument mockingly;
For man will be blotted out, the blithe earth die, the brave sun
Die blind and blacken to the heart:
Yet stones have stood for a thousand years, and pained thoughts
    found
The honey of peace in old poems.

Shine, Perishing Republic

While this America settles in the mould of its vulgarity, heavily
    thickening to empire,
And protest, only a bubble in the molten mass, pops and sighs out,
    and the mass hardens,

I sadly smiling remember that the flower fades to make fruit, the
    fruit rots to make earth.
Out of the mother; and through the spring exultances, ripeness and
    decadence; and home to the mother.

You making haste haste on decay: not blameworthy; life is good,
    be it stubbornly long or suddenly
A mortal splendour: meteors are not needed less than mountains:
    shine, perishing republic.

But for my children, I would have them keep their distance from
    the thickening centre; corruption
Never has been compulsory, when the cities lie at the monster's
    feet there are left the mountains.

And boys, be in nothing so moderate as in love of man, a clever
    servant, insufferable master.
There is the trap that catches noblest spirits, that caught—they say—
    God, when he walked on earth.

Marianne Moore

1887–

After she graduated from Bryn Mawr and Carlisle Commercial College, Marianne Moore taught for a period at the Carlisle Indian School. She later moved to New York, where she was first a librarian and then an editor of the best American magazine of the time, *The Dial*. She published a few of her poems, but modesty forbade book publication until friends surprised her with the publication of *Poems* (1921). She lived in Brooklyn until 1965 when she moved to Greenwich Village, and has steadily produced a corpus of poems and essays, as well as her translation of *The Fables of La Fontaine*.

Poetry

I, too, dislike it: there are things that are important
     beyond all this fiddle.
  Reading it, however, with a perfect contempt for it, one
     discovers in
  it after all, a place for the genuine.
    Hands that can grasp, eyes
    that can dilate, hair that can rise
     if it must, these things are important not because a

high-sounding interpretation can be put upon them but
     because they are
  useful. When they become so derivative as to become
     unintelligible,
  the same thing may be said for all of us, that we
    do not admire what
    we cannot understand: the bat
     holding on upside down or in quest of something
     to

eat, elephants pushing, a wild horse taking a roll, a tireless
     wolf under
  a tree, the immovable critic twitching his skin like a
     horse that feels a flea, the base-

ball fan, the statistician—
    nor is it valid
        to discriminate against 'business documents and

school-books'; all these phenomena are important. One
        must make a distinction
    however: when dragged into prominence by half poets,
        the result is not poetry,
    nor till the poets among us can be
        'literalists of
        the imagination'—above
            insolence and triviality and can present

for inspection, imaginary gardens with real toads in them,
        shall we have
    it. In the meantime, if you demand on the one hand,
    the raw material of poetry in
        all its rawness and
        that which is on the other hand
            genuine, then you are interested in poetry.

What Are Years?

        What is our innocence,
    what is our guilt? All are
    naked, none is safe. And whence
    is courage: the unanswered question,
    the resolute doubt,—
    dumbly calling, deafly listening—that
    in misfortune, even death,
            encourages others
            and in its defeat, stirs

        the soul to be strong? He
    sees deep and is glad, who
        accedes to mortality
    and in his imprisonment, rises
    upon himself as
    the sea in a chasm, struggling to be

free and unable to be,
    in its surrendering
    finds its continuing.

  So he who strongly feels,
behaves. The very bird,
  grown taller as he sings, steels
his form straight up. Though he is captive,
his mighty singing
says, satisfaction is a lowly
thing, how pure a thing is joy.
    This is mortality,
    this is eternity.

The Mind is an Enchanting Thing

  is an enchanted thing
    like the glaze on a
katydid-wing
      subdivided by sun
      till the nettings are legion.
Like Gieseking playing Scarlatti;

like the apteryx-awl
    as a beak, or the
kiwi's rain-shawl
      of haired feathers, the mind
      feeling its way as though blind,
walks along with its eyes on the ground.

It has memory's ear
    that can hear without
having to hear.
      Like the gyroscope's fall,
      truly unequivocal
because trued by regnant certainty,

it is a power of
    strong enchantment. It

[130]

is like the dove-
          neck animated by
          sun; it is memory's eye;
it's conscientious inconsistency.

It tears off the veil; tears
     the temptation, the
mist the heart wears,
          from its eyes,—if the heart
          has a face; it takes apart
dejection. It's fire in the dove-neck's

iridescence, in the
     inconsistencies
of Scarlatti.
          Unconfusion submits
          its confusion to proof; it's
not a Herod's oath that cannot change.

John Crowe Ransom

1888–

A leader of the Southern regionalists, Ransom studied at Vanderbilt and Oxford, where he was a Rhodes Scholar. He returned to teach at Vanderbilt and Kenyon College, where he edited *The Kenyon Review* from 1939 until his retirement in 1958. He is prominent as a critic, with *The World's Body* and *The New Criticism*.

Bells for John Whiteside's Daughter

There was such speed in her little body,
And such lightness in her footfall,
It is no wonder her brown study
Astonishes us all.

Her wars were bruited in our high window.
We looked among orchard trees and beyond,
Where she took arms against her shadow,
Or harried unto the pond

The lazy geese, like a snow cloud
Dripping their snow on the green grass,
Tricking and stopping, sleepy and proud,
Who cried in goose, Alas,

For the tireless heart within the little
Lady with rod that made them rise
From their noon apple-dreams and scuttle
Goose-fashion under the skies!

But now go the bells, and we are ready,
In one house we are sternly stopped
To say we are vexed at her brown study,
Lying so primly propped.

Captain Carpenter

Captain Carpenter rose up in his prime
Put on his pistols and went riding out

But had got wellnigh nowhere at that time
Till he fell in with ladies in a rout.

It was a pretty lady and all her train
That played with him so sweetly but before
An hour she'd taken a sword with all her main
And twined him of his nose for evermore.

Captain Carpenter mounted up one day
And rode straightway into a stranger rogue
That looked unchristian but be that as may
The Captain did not wait upon prologue.

But drew upon him out of his great heart
The other swung against him with a club
And cracked his two legs at the shinny part
And let him roll and stick like any tub.

Captain Carpenter rode many a time
From male and female took he sundry harms
He met the wife of Satan crying 'I'm
The she-wolf bids you shall bear no more arms.'

Their strokes and counters whistled in the wind
I wish he had delivered half his blows
But where she should have made off like a hind
The bitch bit off his arms at the elbows.

And Captain Carpenter parted with his ears
To a black devil that used him in this wise
O Jesus ere his threescore and ten years
Another had plucked out his sweet blue eyes.

Captain Carpenter got up on his roan
And sallied from the gate in hell's despite
I heard him asking in the grimmest tone
If any enemy yet there was to fight?

'To any adversary it is fame
If he risk to be wounded by my tongue

[133]

Or burnt in two beneath my red heart's flame
Such are the perils he is cast among.

'But if he can he has a pretty choice
From an anatomy with little to lose
Whether he cut my tongue and take my voice
Or whether it be my round red heart he choose.'

It was the neatest knave that ever was seen
Stepping in perfume from his lady's bower
Who at this word put in his merry mien
And fell on Captain Carpenter like a tower.

I would not knock old fellows in the dust
But there lay Captain Carpenter on his back
His weapons were the old heart in his bust
And a blade shook between rotten teeth alack.

The rogue in scarlet and grey soon knew his mind
He wished to get his trophy and depart
With gentle apology and touch refined
He pierced him and produced the Captain's heart.

God's mercy rest on Captain Carpenter now
I thought him Sirs an honest gentleman
Citizen husband soldier and scholar enow
Let jangling kites eat of him if they can.

But God's deep curses follow after those
That shore him of his goodly nose and ears
His legs and strong arms at the two elbows
And eyes that had not watered seventy years.

The curse of hell upon the sleek upstart
That got the Captain finally on his back
And took the red red vitals of his heart
And made the kites to whet their beaks clack clack.

Archibald MacLeish

1892–

MacLeish practised law after his graduation from Harvard Law School, and published one book of poems, before he joined the expatriates in Paris in 1923. Later, he worked for *Fortune*, became a speechwriter for President Franklin Roosevelt, was Librarian of Congress and Assistant Secretary of State before he became Boylston Professor at Harvard in 1949. In 1958 his play *J.B.* won the Pulitzer Prize for Drama.

You, Andrew Marvell

And here face down beneath the sun
And here upon earth's noonward height
To feel the always coming on
The always rising of the night

To feel creep up the curving east
The earthy chill of dusk and slow
Upon those under lands the vast
And ever climbing shadow grow

And strange at Ecbatan the trees
Take leaf by leaf the evening strange
The flooding dark about their knees
The mountains over Persia change

And now at Kermanshah the gate
Dark empty and the withered grass
And through the twilight now the late
Few travellers in the westward pass

And Baghdad darken and the bridge
Across the silent river gone
And through Arabia the edge
Of evening widen and steal on

And deepen on Palmyra's street
The wheel rut in the ruined stone
And Lebanon fade out and Crete
High through the clouds and overblown

And over Sicily the air
Still flashing with the landward gulls
And loom and slowly disappear
The sails above the shadowy hulls

And Spain go under and the shore
Of Africa the gilded sand
And evening vanish and no more
The low pale light across that land

Nor now the long light on the sea

And here face downward in the sun
To feel how swift how secretly
The shadow of the night comes on . . .

Phelps Putnam
1894–1948

Putnam published only two collections of verse in his lifetime, and is still unrepresented by a collected volume. He worked in copper mines, and as an editor on the *Atlantic Monthly*.

Hasbrouck and the Rose

Hasbrouck was there and so were Bill
And Smollet Smith the poet, and Ames was there.
After his thirteenth drink, the burning Smith,
Raising his fourteenth trembling in the air,
Said, 'Drink with me, Bill, drink up to the Rose.'
But Hasbrouck laughed like old men in a myth,
Inquiring, 'Smollet, are you drunk? What rose?'
And Smollet said, 'I drunk? It may be so;
Which comes from brooding on the flower, the flower
I mean toward which mad hour by hour
I travel brokenly; and I shall know,
With Hermes and the alchemists—but, hell,
What use is it talking that way to you?
Hard-boiled, unbroken egg, what can you care
For the enfolded passion of the Rose?'
Then Hasbrouck's voice rang like an icy bell:
'Arcane romantic flower, meaning what?
Do you know what it meant? Do I?
We do not know.
Unfolding pungent Rose, the glowing bath
Of ecstasy and clear forgetfulness;
Closing and secret bud one might achieve
By long debauchery—
Except that I have eaten it, and so
There is no call for further lunacy.
In Springfield, Massachusetts, I devoured
The mystic, the improbable, the Rose.
For two nights and a day, rose and rosette
And petal after petal and the heart,

[137]

I had my banquet by the beams
Of four electric stars which shone
Weakly into my room, for there,
Drowning their light and gleaming at my side,
Was the incarnate star
Whose body bore the stigma of the Rose.
And that is all I know about the flower;
I have eaten it—it has disappeared.
There is no Rose.'

Young Smollet Smith let fall his glass; he said,
'Oh Jesus, Hasbrouck, am I drunk or dead?'

E. E. Cummings
1894–1962

Cummings went to France to drive an ambulance in the first war, after his graduation from Harvard, and through a misunderstanding spent considerable time in a French prison, an experience he described in a prose book, *The Enormous Room*. A prolific poet, his innovations are usually typographical and decorative, rather than structural. His satirical verses remain his best. He was active as a painter as well as a poet, and also wrote plays and a volume, *Eimi*, about a visit to Soviet Russia.

'the Cambridge ladies'

the Cambridge ladies who live in furnished souls
are unbeautiful and have comfortable minds
(also, with the church's protestant blessings
daughters, unscented shapeless spirited)
they believe in Christ and Longfellow, both dead,
are invariably interested in so many things—
at the present writing one still finds
delighted fingers knitting for the is it Poles?
perhaps. While permanent faces coyly bandy
scandal of Mrs. N and Professor D
. . . . the Cambridge ladies do not care, above
Cambridge if sometimes in its box of
sky lavender and cornerless, the
moon rattles like a fragment of angry candy

Poem, or Beauty Hurts Mr. Vinal

take it from me kiddo
believe me
my country, 'tis of

you, land of the Cluett
Shirt Boston Garter and Spearmint

[139]

Girl With The Wrigley Eyes(of you
land of the Arrow Ide
and Earl &
Wilson
Collars)of you i
sing: land of Abraham Lincoln and Lydia E. Pinkham,
land above all of Just Add Hot Water And Serve—
from every B. V. D.

let freedom ring

amen. i do however protest, anent the un
-spontaneous and otherwise scented merde which
greets one(Everywhere Why)as divine poesy per
that and this radically defunct periodical. i would
suggest that certain ideas gestures
rhymes, like Gillette Razor Blades
having been used and reused
to the mystical moment of dullness emphatically are
Not To Be Resharpened. (Case in point

if we are to believe these gently O sweetly
melancholy trillers amid the thrillers
these crepuscular violinists among my and your
skyscrapers—Helen & Cleopatra were Just Too Lovely,
The Snail's On The Thorn enter Morn and God's
In His andsoforth

do you get me?)according
to such supposedly indigenous
throstles Art is O World O Life
a formula: example, Turn Your Shirttails Into
Drawers and If It Isn't An Eastman It Isn't A
Kodak therefore my friends let
us now sing each and all fortissimo A-
mer
i

ca, I
love,

You. And there're a
hun-dred-mil-lion-oth-ers, like
all of you successfully if
delicately gelded(or spaded)
gentlemen(and ladies)—pretty

littleliverpill-
hearted-Nujolneeding-There's-A-Reason
americans(who tensetendoned and with
upward vacant eyes, painfully
perpetually crouched, quivering, upon the
sternly allotted sandpile
—how silently
emit a tiny violetflavoured nuisance:Odor?

ono.
comes out like a ribbon lies flat on the brush

'my sweet old etcetera'

 my sweet old etcetera
 aunt lucy during the recent

 war could and what
 is more did tell you just
 what everybody was fighting

 for,
 my sister

 isabel created hundreds
 (and
 hundreds)of socks not to
 mention shirts fleaproof earwarmers
 etcetera wristers etcetera, my
 mother hoped that

 i would die etcetera
 bravely of course my father used

to become hoarse talking about how it was
a privilege and if only he
could meanwhile my

self etcetera lay quietly
in the deep mud et

cetera
(dreaming,
et
    cetera, of
Your smile
eyes knees and of your Etcetera)

F. R. Scott
1899–

A native of Quebec, Scott studied at Oxford and is a professor in the Faculty of Law at McGill. His writing includes essays on national and international politics, but he has been most prominent as a poet and leader of Canadian poets.

Trans Canada

Pulled from our ruts by the made-to-order gale
We sprang upward into a wider prairie
And dropped Regina below like a pile of bones.

Sky tumbled upon us in waterfalls,
But we were smarter than a Skeena salmon
And shot our silver body over the lip of air
To rest in a pool of space
On the top storey of our adventure.

A solar peace
And a six-way choice.

Clouds, now, are the solid substance,
A floor of wool roughed by the wind
Standing in waves that halt in their fall.
A still of troughs.

The plane, our planet,
Travels on roads that are not seen or laid
But sound in instruments on pilots' ears,
While underneath,
The sure wings
Are the everlasting arms of science.

Man, the lofty worm, tunnels his latest clay,
And bores his new career.

This frontier, too, is ours.
This everywhere whose life can only be led
At the pace of a rocket
Is common to man and man,
And every country below is an I land.

The sun sets on its top shelf,
And stars seem farther from our nearer grasp.

I have sat by nights beside a cold lake
And touched things smoother than moonlight on still water,
But the moon on this cloud sea is not human,
And here is no shore, no intimacy,
Only the start of space, the road to suns.

Caring

Caring is loving, motionless,
An interval of more and less
Between the stress and the distress.

After the present falls the past,
After the festival, the fast.
Always the deepest is the last.

This is the circle we must trace,
Not spiralled outward, but a space
Returning to its starting place.

Centre of all we mourn and bless,
Centre of calm beyond excess,
Who cares for caring, has caress.

Hart Crane

1899–1932

Crane left school at sixteen, already a poet of talent. He published in small periodicals and lived mostly in New York, where he pursued dissipation with the same energy he applied to poetry. *White Buildings*, his first and best volume, appeared in 1926. In 1929 he published the first edition of *The Bridge*, a would-be epic which succeeds as a collection of frequently brilliant lyrics. His life was unhappy, and he killed himself in 1932.

Legend

As silent as a mirror is believed
Realities plunge in silence by . . .

I am not ready for repentance;
Nor to match regrets. For the moth
Bends no more than the still
Imploring flame. And tremorous
In the white falling flakes
Kisses are,—
The only worth all granting.

It is to be learned—
This cleaving and this burning,
But only by the one who
Spends out himself again.

Twice and twice
(Again the smoking souvenir,
Bleeding eidolon!) and yet again.
Until the bright logic is won
Unwhispering as a mirror
Is believed.

Then, drop by caustic drop, a perfect cry
Shall string some constant harmony,—

Relentless caper for all those who step
The legend of their youth into the noon.

Repose of Rivers

The willows carried a slow sound,
A sarabande the wind mowed on the mead.
I could never remember
That seething, steady leveling of the marshes
Till age had brought me to the sea.

Flags, weeds. And remembrance of steep alcoves
Where cypresses shared the noon's
Tyranny; they drew me into hades almost.
And mammoth turtles climbing sulphur dreams
Yielded, while sun-silt rippled them
Asunder . . .

How much I would have bartered! the black gorge
And all the singular nestings in the hills
Where beavers learn stitch and tooth.
The pond I entered once and quickly fled—
I remember now its singing willow rim.

And finally, in that memory all things nurse;
After the city that I finally passed
With scalding unguents spread and smoking darts
The monsoon cut across the delta
At gulf gates . . . There, beyond the dykes

I heard wind flaking sapphire, like this summer,
And willows could not hold more steady sound.

The Wine Menagerie

Invariably when wine redeems the sight,
Narrowing the mustard scansions of the eyes,

A leopard ranging always in the brow
Asserts a vision in the slumbering gaze.

Then glozening decanters that reflect the street
Wear me in crescents on their bellies. Slow
Applause flows into liquid cynosures:
—I am conscripted to their shadows' glow.

Against the imitation onyx wainscoting
(Painted emulsion of snow, eggs, yarn, coal, manure)
Regard the forceps of the smile that takes her.
Percussive sweat is spreading to his hair. Mallets,
Her eyes, unmake an instant of the world . . .

What is it in this heap the serpent pries—
Whose skin, facsimile of time, unskeins
Octagon, sapphire transepts round the eyes;
—From whom some whispered carillon assures
Speed to the arrow into feathered skies?

Sharp to the window-pane guile drags a face,
And as the alcove of her jealousy recedes
An urchin who has left the snow
Nudges a cannister across the bar
While August meadows somewhere clasp his brow.

Each chamber, transept, coins some squint,
Remorseless line, minting their separate wills—
Poor streaked bodies wreathing up and out,
Unwitting the stigma that each turn repeals:
Between black tusks the roses shine!

New thresholds, new anatomies! Wine talons
Build freedom up about me and distill
This competence—to travel in a tear
Sparkling alone, within another's will.

Until my blood dreams a receptive smile
Wherein new purities are snared; where chimes
Before some flame of gaunt repose a shell

[147]

Tolled once, perhaps, by every tongue in hell.
—Anguished, the wit that cries out of me:

'Alas,—these frozen billows of your skill!
Invent new dominoes of love and bile . . .
Ruddy, the tooth implicit of the world
Has followed you. Though in the end you know
And count some dim inheritance of sand,
How much yet meets the treason of the snow.

'Rise from the dates and crumbs. And walk away,
Stepping over Holofernes' shins—
Beyond the wall, whose severed head floats by
With Baptist John's. Their whispering begins.

'—And fold your exile on your back again;
Petrushka's valentine pivots on its pin.'

Voyages

I

Above the fresh ruffles of the surf
Bright striped urchins flay each other with sand.
They have contrived a conquest for shell shucks,
And their fingers crumble fragments of baked weed
Gaily digging and scattering.

And in answer to their treble interjections
The sun beats lightning on the waves,
The waves fold thunder on the sand;
And could they hear me I would tell them:

O brilliant kids, frisk with your dog,
Fondle your shells and sticks, bleached
By time and the elements; but there is a line
You must not cross nor ever trust beyond it
Spry cordage of your bodies to caresses
Too lichen-faithful from too wide a breast.
The bottom of the sea is cruel.

II

And yet this great wink of eternity,
Of rimless floods, unfettered leewardings,
Samite sheeted and processioned where
Her undinal vast belly moonward bends,
Laughing the wrapt inflections of our love;

Take this Sea, whose diapason knells
On scrolls of silver snowy sentences,
The sceptred terror of whose sessions rends
As her demeanors motion well or ill,
All but the pieties of lovers' hands.

And onward, as bells off San Salvador
Salute the crocus lustres of the stars,
In these poinsettia meadows of her tides,—
Adagios of islands, O my Prodigal,
Complete the dark confessions her veins spell.

Mark how her turning shoulders wind the hours,
And hasten while her penniless rich palms
Pass superscription of bent foam and wave,—
Hasten, while they are true,—sleep, death, desire,
Close round one instant in one floating flower.

Bind us in time, O Seasons clear, and awe.
O minstrel galleons of Carib fire,
Bequeath us to no earthly shore until
Is answered in the vortex of our grave
The seal's wide spindrift gaze toward paradise.

III

Infinite consanguinity it bears—
This tendered theme of you that light
Retrieves from sea plains where the sky
Resigns a breast that every wave enthrones;
While ribboned water lanes I wind
Are laved and scattered with no stroke
Wide from your side, whereto this hour
The sea lifts, also, reliquary hands.

And so, admitted through black swollen gates
That must arrest all distance otherwise,—
Past whirling pillars and lithe pediments,
Light wrestling there incessantly with light,
Star kissing star through wave on wave unto
Your body rocking!
                    and where death, if shed,
Presumes no carnage, but this single change,—
Upon the steep floor flung from dawn to dawn
The silken skilled transmemberment of song;

Permit me voyage, love, into your hands . . .

The Broken Tower

The bell-rope that gathers God at dawn
Dispatches me as though I dropped down the knell
Of a spent day—to wander the cathedral lawn
From pit to crucifix, feet chill on steps from hell.

Have you not heard, have you not seen that corps
Of shadows in the tower, whose shoulders sway
Antiphonal carillons launched before
The stars are caught and hived in the sun's ray?

The bells, I say, the bells break down their tower;
And swing I know not where. Their tongues engrave
Membrane through marrow, my long-scattered score
Of broken intervals . . . And I, their sexton slave!

Oval encyclicals in canyons heaping
The impasse high with choir. Banked voices slain!
Pagodas, campaniles with reveilles outleaping—
O terraced echoes prostrate on the plain! . . .

And so it was I entered the broken world
To trace the visionary company of love, its voice
An instant in the wind (I know not whither hurled)
But not for long to hold each desperate choice.

My word I poured. But was it cognate, scored
Of that tribunal monarch of the air
Whose thigh embronzes earth, strikes crystal Word
In wounds pledged once to hope—cleft to despair?

The steep encroachments of my blood left me
No answer (could blood hold such a lofty tower
As flings the question true?)—or is it she
Whose sweet mortality stirs latent power?—

And through whose pulse I hear, counting the strokes
My veins recall and add, revived and sure
The angelus of wars my chest evokes:
What I hold healed, original now, and pure . . .

And builds, within, a tower that is not stone
(Not stone can jacket heaven)—but slip
Of pebbles—visible wings of silence sown
In azure circles, widening as they dip

The matrix of the heart, lift down the eye
That shrines the quiet lake and swells a tower . . .
The commodious, tall decorum of that sky
Unseals her earth, and lifts love in its shower.

Allen Tate

1899–

Tate was a student of John Crowe Ransom at Vanderbilt, and was one of the founders of the Fugitives. A teacher, a critic, biographer, novelist and editor, Tate has ranged widely over contemporary literature in America.

Ode to the Confederate Dead

Row after row with strict impunity
The headstones yield their names to the element,
The wind whirrs without recollection;
In the riven troughs the splayed leaves
Pile up, of nature the casual sacrament
To the seasonal eternity of death;
Then driven by the fierce scrutiny
Of heaven to their election in the vast breath,
They sough the rumour of mortality.

Autumn is desolation in the plot
Of a thousand acres where these memories grow
From the inexhaustible bodies that are not
Dead, but feed the grass row after rich row.
Think of the autumns that have come and gone!—
Ambitious November with the humours of the year,
With a particular zeal for every slab,
Staining the uncomfortable angels that rot
On the slabs, a wing chipped here, an arm there:
The brute curiosity of an angel's stare
Turns you, like them, to stone,
Transforms the heaving air
Till plunged to a heavier world below
You shift your sea-space blindly
Heaving, turning like the blind crab.

Dazed by the wind, only the wind
The leaves flying, plunge

You know who have waited by the wall
The twilight certainty of an animal,
Those midnight restitutions of the blood
You know—the immitigable pines, the smoky frieze
Of the sky, the sudden call: you know the rage,
The cold pool left by the mounting flood,
Of muted Zeno and Parmenides.
You who have waited for the angry resolution
Of those desires that should be yours tomorrow,
You know the unimportant shrift of death
And praise the vision
And praise the arrogant circumstance
Of those who fall
Rank upon rank, hurried beyond decision—
Here by the sagging gate, stopped by the wall.

   Seeing, seeing only the leaves
   Flying, plunge and expire

Turn your eyes to the immoderate past,
Turn to the inscrutable infantry rising
Demons out of the earth—they will not last.
Stonewall, Stonewall, and the sunken fields of hemp,
Shiloh, Antietam, Malvern Hill, Bull Run.
Lost in that orient of the thick-and-fast
You will curse the setting sun.

   Cursing only the leaves crying
   Like an old man in a storm

You hear the shout, the crazy hemlocks point
With troubled fingers to the silence which
Smothers you, a mummy, in time.

               The hound bitch
Toothless and dying, in a musty cellar
Hears the wind only.

         Now that the salt of their blood
Stiffens the saltier oblivion of the sea,

Seals the malignant purity of the flood,
What shall we who count our days and bow
Our heads with a commemorial woe
In the ribboned coats of grim felicity,
What shall we say of the bones, unclean,
Whose verdurous anonymity will grow?
The ragged arms, the ragged heads and eyes
Lost in these acres of the insane green?
The gray lean spiders come, they come and go;
In a tangle of willows without light
The singular screech-owl's tight
Invisible lyric seeds the mind
With the furious murmur of their chivalry.

    We shall say only the leaves
    Flying, plunge and expire

We shall say only the leaves whispering
In the improbable mist of nightfall
That flies on multiple wing;
Night is the beginning and the end
And in between the ends of distraction
Waits mute speculation, the patient curse
That stones the eyes, or like the jaguar leaps
For his own image in a jungle pool, his victim.
What shall we say who have knowledge
Carried to the heart? Shall we take the act
To the grave? Shall we, more hopeful, set up the grave
In the house? The ravenous grave?

                        Leave now
The shut gate and the decomposing wall:
The gentle serpent, green in the mulberry bush
Riots with his tongue through the hush—
Sentinel of the grave who counts us all!

Earle Birney

1904–

Birney was born in Calgary, Alberta, and teaches at the University of British Columbia. He has edited *20th Century Canadian Poetry* and a collection of the poems of Malcolm Lowry.

Memory No Servant

but a stubborn master

Eight years ago   weekend in Vera Cruz
It was sugary hot   no doubt
I'm sure my bed was a hammock
cocooned in cheesecloth

Oleander?   There must have been . . .
past the fountains down to the sea
which I rather think was too warm
. . . or were they hibiscus?
Somebody else recalls that the meals
were good   and cheap
I have some colour slides that surprise me
with improbable cascades
of bougainvillea between gold-cups

But what I can be certain not to forget:

    Ten feet from the first bridge
    on the highway north from the town
    a turtle coming up from the Gulf
    Both right wheels ran over its middle
The sound   a crushed carton
    Looking back:—
    the untouched head
ancient   stretched   **and still**
    moving

Looking from Oregon

'And what it watches is not our wars' (Robinson Jeffers)

Far out as I can see
into the crazy dance of light
there are cormorants like little black eyebrows
wriggling and drooping
          but the eye is out of all proportion

Nearer   just beyond the roiling surf
salmon   the young or the sperm-heavy
are being overtaken by bird's neb
sealion's teeth   fisherman's talon

The spent waters
          flecks in this corner of the eyeball
falling past my friend and his two sons
          where they straddle the groin's head
collapse on the beach
          after the long race
from where?   perhaps from Tonkin's gulf
          on the bloodshot edge

There's no good my searching the horizon
          I'm one of those another poet saw
          sitting beside our other ocean
I can't look farther out or in

Yet up here in the wild parsnips and the wind
I know the earth is not holding
tumbles in body-lengths
towards thunderheads and unimaginable Asia

though below me on the frothy rocks
my friend and his two boys
do not look up from fishing

[156]

Richard Eberhart

1904–

Born in Minnesota and educated at Dartmouth, Eberhart attended
Cambridge University, taught at a boy's school in New England
and was a business executive before he accepted a position as
Professor of English at Dartmouth.

The Groundhog

In June, amid the golden fields,
I saw a groundhog lying dead.
Dead lay he; my senses shook,
And mind outshot our naked frailty.
There lowly in the vigorous summer
His form began its senseless change,
And made my senses waver dim
Seeing nature ferocious in him.
Inspecting close his maggots' might
And seething cauldron of his being,
Half with loathing, half with a strange love,
I poked him with an angry stick.
The fever arose, became a flame
And Vigour circumscribed the skies,
Immense energy in the sun,
And through my frame a sunless trembling.
My stick had done nor good nor harm.
Then stood I silent in the day
Watching the object, as before;
And kept my reverence for knowledge
Trying for control, to be still,
To quell the passion of the blood;
Until I had bent down on my knees
Praying for joy in the sight of decay.
And so I left; and I returned
In Autumn strict of eye, to see
The sap gone out of the groundhog,
But the bony sodden hulk remained.
But the year had lost its meaning,

[157

And in intellectual chains
I lost both love and loathing,
Mured up in the wall of wisdom.
Another summer took the fields again
Massive and burning, full of life,
But when I chanced upon the spot
There was only a little hair left,
And bones bleaching in the sunlight
Beautiful as architecture;
I watched them like a geometer,
And cut a walking stick from a birch.
It has been three years, now.
There is no sign of the groundhog.
I stood there in the whirling summer,
My hand capped a withered heart,
And thought of China and of Greece,
Of Alexander in his tent;
Of Montaigne in his tower,
Of Saint Theresa in her wild lament.

The Fury of Aerial Bombardment

You would think the fury of aerial bombardment
Would rouse God to relent; the infinite spaces
Are still silent. He looks on shock-pried faces.
History, even, does not know what is meant.

You would feel that after so many centuries
God would give man to repent; yet he can kill
As Cain could, but with multitudinous will,
No farther advanced than in his ancient furies.

Was man made stupid to see his own stupidity?
Is God by definition indifferent, beyond us all?
Is the eternal truth man's fighting soul
Wherein the Beast ravens in its own avidity?

Of Van Wettering I speak, and Averill,
Names on a list, whose faces I do not recall
But they are gone to early death, who late in school
Distinguished the belt feed lever from the belt holding pawl.

Theodore Roethke
1908–1963

Roethke grew up in Saginaw, Michigan, and attended the University of Michigan. He served as tennis coach at Michigan State, and taught English at various universities, most notably the University of Washington in Seattle. His style changed several times during his brief life as a poet, and to many readers he seemed to be at his best in his posthumous volume. (see pp.24–26.)

Cuttings

Sticks-in-a-drowse droop over sugary loam,
Their intricate stem-fur dries;
But still the delicate slips keep coaxing up water;
The small cells bulge;

One nub of growth
Nudges a sand-crumb loose,
Pokes through a musty sheath
Its pale tendrilous horn.

Orchids

They lean over the path,
Adder-mouthed,
Swaying close to the face,
Coming out, soft and deceptive,
Limp and damp, delicate as a young bird's tongue;
Their fluttery fledgling lips
Move slowly,
Drawing in the warm air.

And at night,
The faint moon falling through whitewashed glass,
The heat going down
So their musky smell comes even stronger

[159]

Drifting down from their mossy cradles:
So many devouring infants!
Soft luminescent fingers,
Lips neither dead nor alive,
Loose ghostly mouths
Breathing.

My Papa's Waltz

The whiskey on your breath
Could make a small boy dizzy;
But I hung on like death:
Such waltzing was not easy.

We romped until the pans
Slid from the kitchen shelf;
My mother's countenance
Could not unfrown itself.

The hand that held my wrist
Was battered on one knuckle;
At every step you missed
My right ear scraped a buckle.

You beat time on my head
With a palm caked hard by dirt,
Then waltzed me off to bed
Still clinging to your shirt.

The Visitant

I

A cloud moved close. The bulk of the wind shifted.
A tree swayed over water.
A voice said:
Stay. Stay by the slip-ooze. Stay.

Dearest tree, I said, may I rest here?
A ripple made a soft reply.

I waited, alert as a dog.
The leech clinging to a stone waited;
And the crab, the quiet breather.

2

Slow, slow as a fish she came,
Slow as a fish coming forward,
Swaying in a long wave;
Her skirts not touching a leaf,
Her white arms reaching towards me.

She came without sound,
Without brushing the wet stones;
In the soft dark of early evening,
She came,
The wind in her hair,
The moon beginning.

3

I woke in the first of morning.
Staring at a tree, I felt the pulse of a stone.
Where's she now, I kept saying.
Where's she now, the mountain's downy girl?
But the bright day had no answer.
A wind stirred in a web of appleworms;
The tree, the close willow, swayed.

I Knew a Woman

I knew a woman, lovely in her bones,
When small birds sighed, she would sigh back at them;
Ah, when she moved, she moved more ways than one:
The shapes a bright container can contain!
Of her choice virtues only gods should speak,
Or English poets who grew up on Greek
(I'd have them sing in chorus, cheek to cheek).

How well her wishes went! She stroked my chin,
She taught me Turn, and Counter-turn, and Stand;

She taught me Touch, that undulant white skin;
I nibbled meekly from her proffered hand;
She was the sickle; I, poor I, the rake,
Coming behind her for her pretty sake
(But what prodigious mowing we did make).

Love likes a gander, and adores a goose:
Her full lips pursed, the errant note to seize;
She played it quick, she played it light and loose;
My eyes, they dazzled at her flowing knees;
Her several parts could keep a pure repose,
Or one hip quiver with a mobile nose
(She moved in circles, and those circles moved).

Let seed be grass, and grass turn into hay:
I'm martyr to a motion not my own;
What's freedom for? To know eternity.
I swear she cast a shadow white as stone.
But who would count eternity in days?
These old bones live to learn her wanton ways:
(I measure time by how a body sways).

The Meadow Mouse

I

In a shoe box stuffed in an old nylon stocking
Sleeps the baby mouse I found in the meadow,
Where he trembled and shook beneath a stick
Till I caught him up by the tail and brought him in,
Cradled in my hand,
A little quaker, the whole body of him trembling,
His absurd whiskers sticking out like a cartoon-mouse,
His feet like small leaves,
Little lizard-feet,
Whitish and spread wide when he tried to struggle away,
Wriggling like a miniscule puppy.

Now he's eaten his three kinds of cheese and drunk from his bottle-
cap watering-trough—

So much he just lies in one corner,
His tail curled under him, his belly big
As his head; his bat-like ears
Twitching, tilting toward the least sound.

Do I imagine he no longer trembles
When I come close to him?
He seems no longer to tremble.

2

But this morning the shoe-box house on the back porch is empty.
Where has he gone, my meadow mouse,
My thumb of a child that nuzzled in my palm?—
To run under the hawk's wing,
Under the eye of the great owl watching from the elm-tree,
To live by courtesy of the shrike, the snake, the tom-cat.

I think of the nestling fallen into the deep grass,
The turtle gasping in the dusty rubble of the highway,
The paralytic stunned in the tub, and the water rising,—
All things innocent, hapless, forsaken.

Journey to the Interior

I

In the long journey out of the self,
There are many detours, washed-out interrupted raw places
Where the shale slides dangerously
And the back wheels hang almost over the edge
At the sudden veering, the moment of turning.
Better to hug close, wary of rubble and falling stones.
The arroyo cracking the road, the wind-bitten buttes, the canyons,
Creeks swollen in midsummer from the flash-flood roaring into the
    narrow valley.
Reeds beaten flat by wind and rain,
Grey from the long winter, burnt at the base in late summer.
—Or the path narrowing,
Winding upward toward the stream with its sharp stones,
The upland of alder and birchtrees,

Through the swamp alive with quicksand,
The way blocked at last by a fallen fir-tree,
The thickets darkening,
The ravines ugly.

2

I remember how it was to drive in gravel,
Watching for dangerous down-hill places, where the wheels whined
    beyond eighty—
When you hit the deep pit at the bottom of the swale,
The trick was to throw the car sideways and charge over the hill,
    full of the throttle.
Grinding up and over the narrow road, spitting and roaring.
A chance? Perhaps. But the road was part of me, and its ditches,
And the dust lay thick on my eyelids,—Who ever wore goggles?—
Always a sharp turn to the left past a barn close to the roadside,
To a scurry of small dogs and a shriek of children,
The highway ribboning out in a straight thrust to the North,
To the sand dunes and fish flies, hanging, thicker than moths,
Dying brightly under the street lights sunk in coarse concrete,
The towns with their high pitted road-crowns and deep gutters,
Their wooden stores of silvery pine and weather-beaten red court-
    houses,
An old bridge below with a buckled iron railing, broken by some
    idiot plunger;
Underneath, the sluggish water running between weeds, broken
    wheels, tires, stones.
And all flows past—
The cemetery with two scrubby trees in the middle of the prairie,
The dead snakes and muskrats, the turtles gasping in the rubble,
The spikey purple bushes in the winding dry creek bed—
The floating hawks, the jackrabbits, the grazing cattle—
I am not moving but they are,
And the sun comes out of a blue cloud over the Tetons,
While, farther away, the heat-lightning flashes.
I rise and fall in the slow sea of a grassy plain,
The wind veering the car slightly to the right,
Whipping the line of white laundry, bending the cottonwoods
    apart,
The scraggly wind-break of a dusty ranch-house.

I rise and fall, and time folds
Into a long moment;
And I hear the lichen speak,
And the ivy advance with its white lizard feet—
On the shimmering road,
On the dusty detour.

3

I see the flower of all water, above and below me, the never receding,
Moving, unmoving in a parched land, white in the moonlight:
The soul at a still-stand,
At ease after rocking the flesh to sleep,
Petals and reflections of petals mixed on the surface of a glassy pool,
And the waves flattening out when the fishermen drag their nets
    over the stones.

In the moment of time when the small drop forms, but does not fall,
I have known the heart of the sun,—
In the dark and light of a dry place,
In a flicker of fire brisked by a dusty wind.
I have heard, in a drip of leaves,
A slight song,
After the midnight cries.
I rehearse myself for this:
The stand at the stretch in the face of death,
Delighting in surface change, the glitter of light on waves,
And I roam elsewhere, my body thinking,
Turning toward the other side of light,
In a tower of wind, a tree idling in air,
Beyond my own echo,
Neither forward nor backward,
Unperplexed, in a place leading nowhere.

As a blind man, lifting a curtain, knows it is morning,
I know this change:
On one side of silence there is no smile;
But when I breathe with the birds,
The spirit of wrath becomes the spirit of blessing,
And the dead begin from their dark to sing in my sleep.

Elizabeth Bishop

1911–

Elizabeth Bishop was born in Massachusetts and has lived for many years in Brazil. She has written little, but her work is consistent. *North and South* appeared in 1946, was reissued with eighteen new poems in 1955, and followed by a new volume in 1965, *Questions of Travel*.

At the Fishhouses

Although it is a cold evening,
down by one of the fishhouses
an old man sits netting,
his net, in the gloaming almost invisible
a dark purple-brown,
and his shuttle worn and polished.
The air smells so strong of codfish
it makes one's nose run and one's eyes water.
The five fishhouses have steeply peaked roofs
and narrow, cleated gangplanks slant up
to storerooms in the gables
for the wheelbarrows to be pushed up and down on.
All is silver: the heavy surface of the sea,
swelling slowly as if considering spilling over,
is opaque, but the silver of the benches,
the lobster pots, and masts, scattered
among the wild jagged rocks,
is of an apparent translucence
like the small old buildings with an emerald moss
growing on their shoreward walls.
The big fish tubs are completely lined
with layers of beautiful herring scales
and the wheelbarrows are similarly plastered
with creamy iridescent coats of mail,
with small iridescent flies crawling on them.
Up on the little slope behind the houses,
set in the sparse bright sprinkle of grass,

[166]

is an ancient wooden capstan,
cracked, with two long bleached handles
and some melancholy stains, like dried blood,
where the ironwork has rusted.

The old man accepts a Lucky Strike.
He was a friend of my grandfather.
We talk of the decline in the population
and of codfish and herring
while he waits for a herring boat to come in.
There are sequins on his vest and on his thumb.
He has scraped the scales, the principal beauty,
from unnumbered fish with that black old knife,
the blade of which is almost worn away.
Down at the water's edge, at the place
where they haul up the boats, up the long ramp
descending into the water, thin silver
tree trunks are laid horizontally
across the gray stones, down and down
at intervals of four or five feet.

Cold dark deep and absolutely clear,
element bearable to no mortal,
to fish and to seals . . . One seal particularly
I have seen here evening after evening.
He was curious about me. He was interested in music;
like me a believer in total immersion,
so I used to sing him Baptist hymns.
I also sang 'A Mighty Fortress Is Our God.'
He stood up in the water and regarded me
steadily, moving his head a little.
Then he would disappear, then suddenly emerge
almost in the same spot, with a sort of shrug
as if it were against his better judgment.
Cold dark deep and absolutely clear,
the clear gray icy water . . . Back, behind us,
the dignified tall firs begin.
Bluish, associating with their shadows,
a million Christmas trees stand
waiting for Christmas. The water seems suspended

above the rounded gray and blue-gray stones.
I have seen it over and over, the same sea, the same,
slightly, indifferently swinging above the stones,
icily free above the stones,
above the stones and then the world.
If you should dip your hand in,
your wrist would ache immediately,
your bones would begin to ache and your hand would burn
as if the water were a transmutation of fire
that feeds on stones and burns with a dark gray flame.
If you tasted it, it would first taste bitter,
then briny, then surely burn your tongue.
It is like what we imagine knowledge to be:
dark, salt, clear, moving, utterly free,
drawn from the cold hard mouth
of the world, derived from the rocky breasts
forever, flowing and drawn, and since
our knowledge is historical, flowing, and flown.

John Berryman

1914–

Berryman was born in Oklahoma and attended Columbia College and Cambridge University. He has taught at numerous universities, most recently the University of Minnesota. *The Dispossessed* appeared in 1948, *Homage to Mistress Bradstreet* in 1956, and *77 Dream Songs* in 1964. He has also written short stories and a biography of Stephen Crane.

Two Dream Songs

I

Henry's pelt was put on sundry walls
where it did much resemble Henry and
them persons was delighted.
Especially his long & glowing tail
by all them was admired, and visitors.
They whistled: This is *it*!

Golden, whilst your frozen daiquiris
whir at midnight, gleams on you his fur
& silky & black.
Mission accomplished, pal.
My molten yellow & moonless bag,
drained, hangs at rest.

Collect in the cold depths barracuda. Ay,
in Sealdah Station some possessionless
hundreds exist & die.
The Chinese communes hum. Two daiquiris
withdrew into a corner of the gorgeous room
and one told the other a lie.

II

In a motion of night they massed nearer my post.
I hummed a short blues. When the stars went out
I studied my weapons system.

Grenades, the portable rack, the yellow spout
of the anthrax-ray: in order. Yes, and most
of my pencils were sharp.

This edge of the galaxy has often seen
a defence so stiff, but it could only go
one way.
—Mr Bones, your troubles give me vertigo,
 & backache. Somehow, when I make your scene,
I cave to feel as if

de roses of dawn & pearls of dusks, made up
by some ol' writer-man, got right forgot
& greennesses of ours.
Springwater grow so thick it gonna clot
and the pleasing ladies cease. I figure, yup,
you is bad powers.

Irving Layton

1912–

A native of Montreal, Layton represents a new generation of Canadian poets whose sources are more American than English. He attended McGill, and teaches in Montreal.

Cat Dying in Autumn

I put the cat outside to die,
Laying her down
Into a rut of leaves
Cold and bloodsoaked;
Her moan
Coming now more quiet
And brief in October's economy
Till the jaws
Opened and shut on no sound.

Behind the wide pane
I watched the dying cat
Whose fur like a veil of air
The autumn wind stirred
Indifferently with the leaves;
Her form (or was it the wind?)
Still breathing—
A surprise of white.

And I was thinking
Of melting snow in spring
Or a strip of gauze
When a sparrow
Dropped down beside it
Leaning his clean beak
Into the hollow;
Then whirred away, his wings,
You may suppose, shuddering.

[171]

Letting me see
From my house
The twisted petal
That fell
Between the ruined paws
To hold or play with,
And the tight smile
Cats have for meeting death.

Misunderstanding

I placed
my hand
upon
her thigh.

By the way
she moved
away
I could see
her devotion
to literature
was not
perfect.

Chokecherries

The sun's gift—

but the leaves a sickly green;
the more exposed curling, showing
a bleached white, many with ragged
holes;
Caterpillars have been
here
sliding their slow destructive bodies
over them.

[172]

I think of them, the leaves, as hoplites
or as anything ingloriously
useful,
suffering, dying . . .

But the chokecherries,
ah;
Still, the leaves' sacrifice
is acrid on the tongue.

Robert Lowell

1917–

Lowell was born in Boston, of the Boston Lowells, cousin of Amy, great-grandnephew of James Russell. He evaded his background by transferring to Kenyon College (and John Crowe Ransom) after a year at Harvard, by converting for some years to Roman Catholicism, and by marrying in succession two southern novelists. He spent time in jail during the Second World War, because of his refusal to serve in any capacity. His Catholicism, in his first volume, *Lord Weary's Castle*, is considerably Calvinist. His confessional free verse, in *Life Studies* and *For the Union Dead*, was extremely influential on American poetry of the 60's, and highly successful, as were his semi-translations, collected as *Imitations*, and his verse plays, *Old Glory*. He is generally considered the best producing American poet.

New Year's Day

Again and then again . . . the year is born
To ice and death, and it will never do
To skulk behind storm-windows by the stove
To hear the postgirl sounding her French horn
When the thin tidal ice is wearing through.
Here is the understanding not to love
Each other, or tomorrow that will sieve
Our resolutions. While we live, we live

To snuff the smoke of victims. In the snow
The kitten heaved its hindlegs, as if fouled,
And died. We bent it in a Christmas box
And scattered blazing weeds to scare the crow
Until the snake-tailed sea-winds coughed and howled
For alms outside the church whose double locks
Wait for St. Peter, the distorted key.
Under St. Peter's bell the parish sea

Swells with its smelt into the burlap shack
Where Joseph plucks his hand-lines like a harp,
And hears the fearful *Puer natus est*
Of Circumcision, and relives the wrack
And howls of Jesus whom he holds. How sharp
The burden of the Law before the beast:
Time and the grindstone and the knife of God.
The Child is born in blood, O child of blood.

The Ghost

(*After Sextus Propertius*)

A ghost is someone: death has left a hole
For the lead-coloured soul to beat the fire:
 Cynthia leaves her dirty pyre
  And seems to coil herself and roll
   Under my canopy,
Love's stale and public playground, where I lie
And fill the run-down empire of my bed.
I see the street, her potter's field, is red
And lively with the ashes of the dead;

But she no longer sparkles off in smoke:
It is the body carted to the gate
 Last Friday, when the sizzling grate
  Left its charred furrows on her smock
   And ate into her hip.
A black nail dangles from a finger-tip
And Lethe oozes from her nether lip.
Her thumb-bones rattle on her brittle hands,
As Cynthia stamps and hisses and demands:

'Sextus, has sleep already washed away
Your manhood? You forget the window-sill
 My sliding wore to slivers? Day
  Would break before the Seven Hills
   Saw Cynthia retreat
And climb your shoulders to the knotted sheet.

You shouldered me and galloped on bare feet
To lay me by the crossroads. Have no fear:
Notus, who snatched your promise, has no ear.

'But why did no one call in my deaf ear?
Your calling would have gained me one more day.
   Sextus, although you ran away
   You might have called and stopped my bier
      A second by your door.
No tears drenched a black toga for your whore
When broken tilestones bruised her face before
The Capitol. Would it have strained your purse
To scatter ten cheap roses on my hearse?

'The State will make Pompilia's Chloris burn:
I knew her secret when I kissed the skull
   Of Pluto in the tainted bowl.
   Let Nomas burn her books and turn
      Her poisons into gold:
The finger-prints upon the potsherd told
Her love. You let a slut, whose body sold
To Thracians, liquefy my golden bust
In the coarse flame that crinkled me to dust.

'If Chloris' bed has left you with your head,
Lover, I think you'll answer my arrears:
   My nurse is getting on in years,
   See that she gets a little bread—
      She never clutched your purse;
See that my little humpback hears no curse
From her close-fisted friend. But burn the verse
You bellowed half a lifetime in my name:
Why should you feed me to the fires of fame?

'I will not hound you, much as you have earned
It, Sextus: I shall reign in your four books—
   I swear this by the Hag who looks
   Into my heart where it was burned:
      Propertius, I kept faith;
If not, may serpents suck my ghost to death

And spit it with their forked and killing breath
Into the Styx where Agamemnon's wife
Founders in the green circles of her life.

'Beat the sycophant ivy from my urn,
That twists its binding shoots about my bones
    Where apple-sweetened Anio drones
    Through orchards that will never burn
        While honest Herakles,
My patron, watches. Anio, you will please
Me if you whisper upon sliding knees:
"Propertius, Cynthia is here:
She shakes her blossoms when my waters clear."

'You cannot turn your back upon a dream,
For phantoms have their reasons when they come:
    We wander midnights: then the numb
    Ghost wades from the Lethean stream;
        Even the foolish dog
Stops its hell-raising mouths and casts its clog;
At cock-crow Charon checks us in his log.
Others can have you, Sextus; I alone
Hold: and I grind your manhood bone on bone.'

After the Surprising Conversions

September twenty-second, Sir: today
I answer. In the latter part of May,
Hard on our Lord's Ascension, it began
To be more sensible. A gentleman
Of more than common understanding, strict
In morals, pious in behaviour, kicked
Against our goad. A man of some renown,
An useful, honoured person in the town,
He came of melancholy parents; prone
To secret spells, for years they kept alone—
His uncle, I believe, was killed of it:
Good people, but of too much or little wit.
I preached one Sabbath on a text from Kings;

He showed concernment for his soul. Some things
In his experience were hopeful. He
Would sit and watch the wind knocking a tree
And praise this countryside our Lord has made.
Once when a poor man's heifer died, he laid
A shilling on the doorsill; though a thirst
For loving shook him like a snake, he durst
Not entertain much hope of his estate
In heaven. Once we saw him sitting late
Behind his attic window by a light
That guttered on his Bible; through that night
He meditated terror, and he seemed
Beyond advice or reason, for he dreamed
That he was called to trumpet Judgment Day
To Concord. In the latter part of May
He cut his throat. And though the coroner
Judged him delirious, soon a noisome stir
Palsied our village. At Jehovah's nod
Satan seemed more let loose amongst us: God
Abandoned us to Satan, and he pressed
Us hard, until we thought we could not rest
Till we had done with life. Content was gone.
All the good work was quashed. We were undone.
The breath of God had carried out a planned
And sensible withdrawal from this land;
The multitude, once unconcerned with doubt,
Once neither callous, curious nor devout,
Jumped at broad noon, as though some peddler groaned
At it in its familiar twang: 'My friend,
Cut your own throat. Cut your own throat. Now! Now!'
September twenty-second, Sir, the bough
Cracks with the unpicked apples, and at dawn
The small-mouth bass breaks water, gorged with spawn.

Waking in the Blue

The night attendant, a B.U. sophomore,
rouses from the mare's-nest of his drowsy head
propped on *The Meaning of Meaning*.

He catwalks down our corridor.
Azure day
makes my agonized blue window bleaker.
Crows maunder on the petrified fairway.
Absence! My heart grows tense
as though a harpoon were sparring for the kill.
(This is the house for the 'mentally ill.')

What use is my sense of humour?
I grin at Stanley, now sunk in his sixties,
once a Harvard all-American fullback,
(if such were possible!)
still hoarding the build of a boy in his twenties,
as he soaks, a ramrod
with the muscle of a seal
in his long tub,
vaguely urinous from the Victorian plumbing.
A kingly granite profile in a crimson golf-cap,
worn all day, all night,
he thinks only of his figure,
of slimming on sherbet and ginger ale—
more cut off from words than a seal.
This is the way day breaks in Bowditch Hall at McLean's:
the hooded night lights bring out 'Bobbie,'
Porcellian '29,
a replica of Louis XVI
without the wig—
redolent and roly-poly as a sperm whale,
as he swashbuckles about in his birthday suit
and horses at chairs.

These victorious figures of bravado ossified young.

In between the limits of day,
hours and hours go by under the crew haircuts
and slightly too little nonsensical bachelor twinkle
of the Roman Catholic attendants.
(There are no Mayflower
screwballs in the Catholic Church.)

[179]

After a hearty New England breakfast,
I weigh two hundred pounds
this morning. Cock of the walk,
I strut in my turtle-necked French sailor's jersey
before the metal shaving mirrors,
and see the shaky future grow familiar
in the pinched, indigenous faces
of these thoroughbred mental cases,
twice my age and half my weight.
We are all old-timers,
each of us holds a locked razor.

Colonel Shaw and the Massachusetts' 54th

'Relinquunt omnia servare rem publicam.'

The old South Boston Aquarium stands
in a Sahara of snow now. Its broken windows are boarded.
The bronze weathervane cod has lost half its scales.
The air tanks are dry.

Once my nose crawled like a snail on the glass;
my hand tingled
to burst the bubbles
drifting from the noses of the cowed, compliant fish.

My hand draws back. I often sigh still
for the dark downward and vegetating kingdom
of the fish and reptile. One morning last March,
I pressed against the new barbed and galvanized

fence on the Boston Common. Behind their cage,
yellow dinosaur steamshovels were grunting
as they cropped up tons of mush and grass
to gouge their underworld garage.

Parking-spaces luxuriate like civic
sandpiles in the heart of Boston.
A girdle of orange, Puritan-pumpkin coloured girders
braces the tingling Statehouse,

shaking over the excavations, as it faces Colonel Shaw
and his bell-cheeked Negro infantry
on St. Gaudens' shaking Civil War relief,
propped by a plank splint against the garage's earthquake.

Two months after marching through Boston,
half the regiment was dead;
at the dedication,
William James could almost hear the bronze Negroes breathe.

Their monument sticks like a fishbone
in the City's throat.
Its Colonel is as lean
as a compass-needle.

He has an angry wrenlike vigilance,
a greyhound's gentle tautness;
he seems to wince at pleasure,
and suffocate for privacy.

He is out of bounds now. He rejoices in man's lovely,
peculiar power to choose life and die—
when he leads his black soldiers to death,
he cannot bend his back.

On a thousand small town New England greens,
the old white churches hold their air
of sparse, sincere rebellion; frayed flags
quilt the graveyards of the Grand Army of the Republic.

The stone statues of the abstract Union Soldier
grow slimmer and younger each year—
wasp-waisted, they doze over muskets
and muse through their sideburns . . .

Shaw's father wanted no monument
except the ditch,
where his son's body was thrown
and lost with his 'niggers.'

[181]

The ditch is nearer.
There are no statues for the last war here;
on Boyleston Street, a commercial photograph
shows Hiroshima boiling

over a Mosler Safe, the 'Rock of Ages'
that survived the blast. Space is nearer.
When I crouch to my television set,
the drained faces of Negro children rise like balloons.

Colonel Shaw
is riding on his bubble,
he waits
for the blessed break.

The Aquarium is gone. Everywhere,
giant finned cars nose forward like fish;
a savage servility
slides by on grease.

Richard Wilbur

1921–

A native of New Jersey, Wilbur attended Amherst College, and, after service in the Second World War, graduate school at Harvard. He has taught at Harvard, Wellesley and now at Wesleyan University. His precise diction and the elegance of his thinking have won him a particular place in contemporary American poetry.

Years-End

Now winter downs the dying of the year,
And night is all a settlement of snow;
From the soft street the rooms of houses show
A gathered light, a shapen atmosphere,
Like frozen-over lakes whose ice is thin
And still allows some stirring down within.

I've known the wind by water banks to shake
The late leaves down, which frozen where they fell
And held in ice as dancers in a spell
Fluttered all winter long into a lake;
Graved on the dark in gestures of descent,
They seemed their own most perfect monument.

There was perfection in the death of ferns
Which laid their fragile cheeks against the stone
A million years. Great mammoths overthrown
Composedly have made their long sojourns,
Like palaces of patience, in the gray
And changeless lands of ice. And at Pompeii

The little dog lay curled and did not rise
But slept the deeper as the ashes rose
And found the people incomplete, and froze
The random hands, the loose unready eyes
Of men expecting yet another sun
To do the shapely thing they had not done.

These sudden ends of time must give us pause.
We fray into the future, rarely wrought
Save in the tapestries of afterthought.
More time, more time. Barrages of applause
Come muffled from a buried radio.
The New-year bells are wrangling with the snow.

Juggler

A ball will bounce, but less and less. It's not
A light-hearted thing, resents its own resilience.
Falling is what it loves, and the earth falls
So in our hearts from brilliance,
Settles and is forgot.
It takes a sky-blue juggler with five red balls

To shake our gravity up. Whee, in the air
The balls roll round, wheel on his wheeling hands,
Learning the ways of lightness, alter to spheres
Grazing his finger ends,
Cling to their courses there,
Swinging a small heaven about his ears.

But a heaven is easier made of nothing at all
Than the earth regained, and still and sole within
The spin of worlds, with a gesture sure and noble
He reels that heaven in,
Landing it ball by ball,
And trades it all for a broom, a plate, a table.

Oh, on his toe the table is turning, the broom's
Balancing up on his nose, and the plate whirls
On the tip of the broom! Damn, what a show, we cry:
The boys stamp, and the girls
Shriek, and the drum booms
And all comes down, and he bows and says good-bye.

If the juggler is tired now, if the broom stands
In the dust again, if the table starts to drop
Through the daily dark again, and though the plate

Lies flat on the table top,
For him we batter our hands
Who has won for once over the world's weight.

In the Elegy Season

Haze, char, and the weather of All Souls':
A giant absence mopes upon the trees:
Leaves cast in casual potpourris
Whisper their scents from pits and cellar-holes.

Or brewed in gulleys, steeped in wells, they spend
In chilly steam their last aromas, yield
From shallow hells a revenance of field
And orchard air. And now the envious mind

Which could not hold the summer in my head
While bounded by that blazing circumstance
Parades these barrens in a golden trance,
Remembering the wealthy season dead,

And by an autumn inspiration makes
A summer all its own. Green boughs arise
Through all the boundless backward of the eyes,
And the soul bathes in warm conceptual lakes.

Less proud than this, my body leans an ear
Past cold and colder weather after wings'
Soft commotion, the sudden race of springs,
The goddess' tread heard on the dayward stair,

Longs for the brush of the freighted air, for smells
Of grass and cordial lilac, for the sight
Of green leaves building into the light
And azure water hoisting out of wells.

Beasts

Beasts in their major freedom
Slumber in peace tonight. The gull on his ledge

[185]

Dreams in the guts of himself the moon-plucked waves below,
    And the sunfish leans on a stone, slept
        By the lyric water;

        In which the spotless feet
    Of deer make dulcet splashes, and to which
The ripped mouse, safe in the owl's talon, cries
    Concordance. Here there is no such harm
        And no such darkness

        As the selfsame moon observes
    Where, warped in window-glass, it sponsors now
The werewolf's painful change. Turning his head away
    On the sweaty bolster, he tries to remember
        The mood of manhood,

        But lies at last, as always,
    Letting it happen, the fierce fur soft to his face,
Hearing with sharper ears the wind's exciting minors,
    The leaves' panic, and the degradation
        Of the heavy streams.

        Meantime, at high windows
    Far from thicket and pad-fall, suitors of excellence
Sigh and turn from their work to construe again the painful
    Beauty of heaven, the lucid moon
        And the risen hunter,

        Making such dreams for men
    As told will break their hearts as always, bringing
Monsters into the city, crows on the public statues,
    Navies fed to the fish in the dark
        Unbridled waters.

STIRLING COUNTY LIBRARY

Index of Titles and First Lines

STIRLING DISTRICT LIBRARY